PCK

FOR ENGLISH LANGUAGE TEACHERS

英 语 教 师 专 业 素 养 丛 书

丛书主编

顾永琦（新西兰）
Peter Yongqi Gu

余国兴
Guoxing Yu

Teaching English for Specific Purposes

如何教专门用途英语

Jean Parkinson（英） 著

外语教学与研究出版社
FOREIGN LANGUAGE TEACHING AND RESEARCH PRESS
北京 BEIJING

京权图字：01-2023-0270

图书在版编目（CIP）数据

如何教专门用途英语 = Teaching English for Specific Purposes：英文 ／
（英）琼·帕金森（Jean Parkinson）著. —— 北京 ：外语教学与研究出版社，
2023.3
  （英语教师专业素养丛书 ／ 余国兴等主编）
  ISBN 978-7-5213-4292-5

Ⅰ. ①如… Ⅱ. ①琼… Ⅲ. ①英语－教学研究－英文 Ⅳ. ①H319.3

中国国家版本馆 CIP 数据核字 (2023) 第 035253 号

出 版 人　王　芳
项目策划　姚　虹
责任编辑　徐　宁
责任校对　都楠楠
装帧设计　郭　莹
出版发行　外语教学与研究出版社
社　　址　北京市西三环北路 19 号（100089）
网　　址　https://www.fltrp.com
印　　刷　三河市北燕印装有限公司
开　　本　650×980　1/16
印　　张　13
版　　次　2023 年 4 月第 1 版　2023 年 4 月第 1 次印刷
书　　号　ISBN 978-7-5213-4292-5
定　　价　31.00 元

如有图书采购需求，图书内容或印刷装订等问题，侵权、盗版书籍等线索，请拨打以下电话或关注官方服务号：
客服电话: 400 898 7008
官方服务号: 微信搜索并关注公众号"外研社官方服务号"
外研社购书网址: https://fltrp.tmall.com

物料号: 342920001

记载人类文明
沟通世界文化
www.fltrp.com

SERIES EDITORS' PREFACE

Pedagogical content knowledge for English language teachers is a series that aims to provide a comprehensive knowledge base for busy classroom teachers. As the name suggests, the series covers issues related to the nature of language competence and how this competence is best taught, learned and assessed. It is hoped that, armed with this broad range of pedagogical content knowledge, ESL/EFL teachers will be able to meaningfully interpret the targets of teaching, learning and assessment, diagnose and solve problems in the teaching process, and grow professionally in the meantime.

The series includes the following seven broad areas:
1) Principles of language teaching
2) Curriculum and targets of teaching
3) Teaching language skills and knowledge
4) Teaching methodology and teaching tools
5) Testing and assessment
6) Language learning
7) Teacher as researcher

Unlike other books that aim for a similar knowledge base, this series attempts to be a digest version that bridges the gap between theories and practices. It also aims to offer easy reading and inexpensive texts that teachers will find easily accessible and applicable. To achieve these aims, all books in this series are written in simple English or Chinese. Each book in this series is authored by an acknowledged authority on the topic. It includes a brief introduction to theories plus a brief review of major research findings. The main text, however, focuses on how the theories and research can be applied to the ESL/EFL classroom.

In addition to the print copy for each book, an e-book version will also be available. Short video clips may also be made available at the publisher's website where some authors introduce their books.

Besides English language teachers who teach ESL/EFL at secondary and primary schools, target readership of this series also includes trainee teachers on short and intensive training programmes. Pre-service teachers who are studying for their MA in TESOL/Applied Linguistics and Year 3/4 English majors who aspire to be English language teachers should find the series very useful as well.

If English language teaching is to be useful at all, we cannot dwell on general English language teaching at primary, secondary and tertiary levels all the time. Learners need to aim for the final target use in specific domains and for specific purposes. This book is a timely addition on teaching English for Specific Purposes (ESP). It focuses on the need for a move from general English language teaching to teaching ESP. In this book, Dr Parkinson presents a succinct introduction to needs analysis, curriculum design, materials development, and the assessment of ESP. English language teachers in vocational schools and at tertiary level will find the book relevant. Even teachers in regular secondary schools will find the perspective refreshing.

Peter Yongqi Gu and Guoxing Yu
Series Editors

PREFACE

This book is for English teachers who are currently teaching English for Specific Purposes (ESP) to tertiary students, or who are interested in moving to teaching English for Specific Purposes. It is also for high school English teachers whose students currently study one or more of their content subjects in English, or whose students will move into tertiary studies or employment where they will need to use English for a specific purpose.

You may be teaching an English for Specific Purposes course or have taught one in the past. Or you may be teaching an English for Academic Purposes (EAP) course, which you or your institution is thinking of altering to make it more specific to the students' disciplinary interests. This book asks you to draw on this experience or, if you have not had first-hand experience, to imagine yourself working in an English for Specific Purposes context in the future. The book discusses how English for Specific Purposes is different from general English language teaching (Chapter 1). It provides opportunities to consider key issues in English for Specific Purposes research as a way of informing practical decisions you would face if you were teaching an ESP course. It asks you to investigate the specific needs of a specific group.

As in most TESOL situations, the first questions you would ask yourself are likely to be: Who are my students, what purpose will they be using this language for and what are their needs? In the first part of the book (Chapters 2-3), you will identify a particular group of students and their specific language needs. While reading the book, you are invited to orient your thinking to a particular specific purposes language teaching/learning situation. If you are not teaching or have not previously taught in a specific purposes context, please use this book to investigate one.

Although secondary school students usually have general English needs rather than specific English needs, in some cases ESP teachers will cater to the specific needs of secondary students. One example is students studying carpentry, poultry science or engineering at a vocational school; another example is the language needs of secondary students studying physics, biology or geography.

Chapter 2 focuses awareness on the various facets of a course which need to be taken into account in relation to the learners' purpose. It will guide you in designing a needs analysis. If put into practice, this will give you both theoretical insights and practical skills in finding out information which is relevant to course design decisions and then drawing appropriate conclusions from it. If you are not working in a specific purposes context, you will need to identify such a context which you can investigate. Examples might be to investigate the following specific contexts:

Specific academic purposes
- Chinese engineering students preparing to study abroad in English
- Chinese medical students doing an English for Medical Purposes course
- Maritime English for students at a Chinese university
- Chinese business students in China who need to read English texts

Specific occupational purposes
- Employees of an international trade company in China who need to communicate with customers abroad
- Chinese engineers in China who need to communicate in English with international clients
- People working in China in the tourism industry – e.g. as tour guides or hotel receptionists – who need to communicate with foreign tourists
- Chinese students studying for a pilot's licence
- The English language needs of a Chinese artist who markets their work internationally on the internet

Chapter 3 extends the focus on needs analysis introduced in Chapter 2 by looking specifically at qualitative methods of needs analysis such as interviews and observation. Chapter 4 looks at curriculum development in ESP. Chapter 5 considers different approaches to curriculum design, or different teaching methods in ESP. Chapters 6 and 7 focus in greater depth on the language that students acquire in ESP courses. This includes the discipline-specific features such as vocabulary, and the discourse features of discipline-specific texts and genres. Chapter 8 considers materials development in ESP. Chapter 9 concerns assessment in ESP, and how to assess language skills that are specific to the studies or occupation of the students.

CONTENTS

Chapter 1

What is English for Specific Purposes?

Pre-reading questions

1) What is the difference between general purposes English courses and specific purposes English courses?
2) What are the benefits of a specific purposes approach?
3) What are the characteristics of specific purposes students: needs, age, occupation, and field of study?

1.1 Introduction

Most foreign language teaching seeks to teach students to use the foreign language for a wide range of 'general' purposes. One purpose is reading and writing all sorts of different texts in the language; this includes reading and writing for academic purposes, writing emails, as well as reading newspapers or even street signs in the foreign language. Another purpose is having conversations in the foreign language, such as meetings or phone calls, or exchange of dialogues during international travel or study abroad.

However, many learners have a need to use the foreign language for a narrow range of purposes. Their reasons for learning the language can be quite specific. English for Specific Purposes may be focused on academic purposes for a particular group of students (e.g. law students), on professional purposes (e.g. medical doctors) or on occupational purposes (e.g. airline pilots). As an English teacher teaching students who are studying English for a specific rather than a general purpose, your students might be learning the language for many different reasons. They might not be interested in learning to use the language in ways that are not relevant to their own specific purpose. Some of these specific purposes are:

- Maybe they want to study a specific discipline in English either in China or in a foreign country.
- They might be studying in China, in Chinese, but need to read textbooks and articles on their discipline in English.

- They might do business internationally and need to write emails about their business in English and speak English on the phone.
- They might want to publish their research in English so that it will have an international readership.
- They might be airline pilots who need to communicate at a high level of accuracy and in a highly restricted variety of English with air traffic controllers in airports all over the world.
- Perhaps they work for a call centre and need to speak to people in other countries who respond better to them if their language is similar to their own.
- They might even be going on holiday abroad and want to be able to check into accommodation, and buy train tickets, meals etc.

However, the following contexts are not English for Specific Purposes contexts:

- An EAP/IELTS course catering to students in a wide range of disciplines. If you are teaching in this context, select students in one particular discipline, profession or context and investigate what a specific purposes response to their needs would be.
- Usually, we would not regard a primary school classroom as a specific purposes context. The students in such classrooms have language needs that are broad and not confined to a specific purpose. However, in some cases it is possible to focus on the needs that primary students have to learn specific purposes language (see Chapter 7).

In this introduction, I will start by sharing my own experience of teaching language for specific purposes. Like some of the English for Specific Purposes teachers described by Basturkmen (2010, pp.3-5), my primary degree was not in TESOL or ESP. I originally studied biology before doing an English literature degree. I then became an English teacher in a school where the students spoke English as their second language. This led to further studies in TESOL. I later became an English teacher of tertiary science students for whom English was their second language. I was therefore able to draw on my own experience as a science student. Science students seldom write essays; more usually they write laboratory reports instead. When they do write essays, these are descriptive essays rather than the discursive essays I had learnt to write in my studies in English literature. By talking to scientist colleagues, I came to realise that scientists place great weight on measurement and conveying an assessment of the reliability of that measurement. By questioning scientists, analysing their texts and reading research on science texts, I learnt some of the values, behaviour and world view of the science community as well as the grammar and structure of its texts.

Later in my career, I was asked to design an English for Specific Purposes course for engineering students. In contrast to my experience of teaching ESP to science students, I have no background in engineering, so to understand engineering culture – how engineers work together and what they regard as important – as well as the spoken and written productions of engineers, I worked with three engineers: civil, mechanical and chemical. I read many student reports which were regarded as good ones by my engineer informants. I found that to prepare engineering students for their future working life as engineers, they work in teams on projects (project-based learning). A key written output is the design report, and a key oral form is the design presentation; these are often produced in teams. In marked contrast to my own literacy background, collaborative writing and oral presentations are important, based on the key values of design and project-oriented teamwork. Without the insights of my informants, I would not have known this. Engineering students do not write essays, so a 'general' English course would be inappropriate, teaching them ways of writing and values they have no need for, and neglecting those they need.

(Task 1.1)

> Share your experience with a partner, or write down your thoughts about the following:
>
> 1. Have you ever taught in a situation where students were learning language for a specific purpose? Describe the situation, the learners' needs and how you feel you met these (or in what ways you feel you/the course failed to do so).
> 2. Have you had experience learning language for a specific purpose? Describe the situation, your needs, and how the learning situation you were in met these (or did not do so).

In considering the difference between ELT and ESP, Basturkmen (2010, p.7) distinguishes between internal goals, which are confined to the classroom, and external goals, which focus on language use outside of the classroom. It is the latter that is a primary focus of ESP.

1.2 The defining features of English for Specific Purposes

Dudley-Evans and St John (1998, p.4) list both the absolute characteristics of ESP (essential in any ESP course) and the variable characteristics (usually but not always present in an ESP course).

1. Absolute characteristics of ESP

a) ESP is designed to meet specific needs of the learners;

b) ESP makes use of the underlying methodologies and activities of the discipline it serves;

c) ESP is centred on the language (register), skills, discourse and genre appropriate to these activities.

2. Variable characteristics of ESP

d) ESP may be related to or designed for specific disciplines;

e) ESP may use, in specific teaching situations, a different methodology from that of general English;

f) ESP is likely to be designed for adult learners, either at a tertiary-level institution or in a professional work situation. It could, however, be for learners at secondary school level;

g) ESP is generally designed for intermediate or advanced students. Most ESP courses assume some basic knowledge of the language system, but it can be used with beginners.

Point (a) above draws on the ideas of Hutchinson and Waters (1987) who place the learning needs of the students as central to an ESP course. A focus on these learning needs is essential in an ESP course, because the point of ESP is to help learners cope with the language needed to study their courses or do their job.

Point (b) above may be surprising. Why would ESP courses use the methodologies and activities of the students' discipline? The answer lies in the fact that the language that students need to learn, mentioned in (c) above, is often situated in these methodologies and activities. For example, for a science student to learn to write a laboratory report, they need to do some experimental work so they can report on it; for an engineering student to write a design report, they need to design something; for a nursing student or medical student to practise talking to patients, a good way is for them to talk to someone role-playing a patient. Similarly, a trainee hotel receptionist will benefit from talking on the phone or face to face with someone role-playing a visitor to a hotel. Employees of an international trade company will benefit from responding to authentic emails, or role-playing telephone conversations or meetings with clients. This accounts for (e) above, the fact that quite different methodologies might be used in ESP than in general English classes.

Points (f) and (g) above relate to learner characteristics and suggest that ESP can be used for a much wider group of learners than is often assumed. As indicated in Point (g), although most ESP students have at least intermediate proficiency, beginners can also have language learning needs. Examples are tourists preparing to visit a country, who might know very little of the language, as well as migrants or refugees to a country who need to prepare themselves to find a job. Jasso-Aguilar (1999) and Edwards (2019) both investigated the needs of low proficiency migrants working as cleaners. Similarly, although most ESP students will be engaged in tertiary studies or in employment, secondary students who are learning various disciplines (e.g. physics, catering, agricultural studies) may also have special purposes needs.

1.3 Why specificity?

In the past, most universities and other tertiary institutions focused on teaching general English courses to their students. However, more recently a focus on ESP courses has developed in many countries around the world, including China.

Task 1.2

Discuss with your partner:
1. What reasons would a teacher or an institution have for choosing a general English course?
2. What reasons would they have for choosing a specific English course?

Hyland (2002b) discusses arguments that have been put forward in favour of a general approach to teaching language. He counters these arguments, stating his own preference for meeting the specific needs of students, and being as specific as we can be in our teaching. Hyland quotes Spack (1988), who points out that most language teachers lack expertise in subject-specific language. This can indeed be a problem, because as Basturkmen (2010, p.8) notes, English for Specific Purposes is concerned with language that is outside the normal repertoire of the average native speaker. The question here is whether English teachers are willing to investigate and learn about the subject-specific language of their students. Instead, Spack (1988) proposes that subject specialists should teach the specific language of their discipline. However, in general, subject specialists prioritise the teaching of the content of their discipline. They also feel that it is not their job to teach language, and most of them do not have the skills to do so. In addition, those already working in occupations do not have teachers as university or college students do. They have to pick up the specific language from their colleagues, and this might take a long time. To solve this problem, in which neither the English teacher nor the subject teacher has the skills to teach specific language, English for Specific Purposes teachers can work together with subject teachers to become familiar with the specialised language and literacy of their students' discipline or profession.

A second argument in favour of a more general approach suggests that there is a 'common core' of skills and forms of language that are generic across disciplines, professions and purposes. However, it is not clear whether a 'common core' can be identified. Johns (1997) says that academic writing displays explicitness, intertextuality, objectivity, emotional neutrality, appropriate genre and a disciplinary vision. She points out, however, that these features are achieved differently in each discipline. Even the meaning and use of apparently common grammatical forms are context dependent, so focusing on specific varieties of language is essential.

These two sets of arguments appear to be based on different ideas of what language and literacy are. Spack's idea of literacy is a more unitary notion of literacy in which we can acquire and hone the principles of rhetoric and use these in a range of contexts and for a variety of uses. Hyland speaks from a tradition that regards literacy as multiple in a range of ways reflective of different discourse communities that expect, understand and recognise:

- Different value systems
- Different ideas of what constitutes a convincing argument
- Different ways of packaging information within the clause and the text
- Different ranges of lexis
- Different genres, both spoken and written

Task 1.3

With a partner, or on your own, consider both sides of the argument presented by Hyland:

1. On the 'general' side of the argument, try to outline what the 'common core'/general principles are that students can learn in an English for General Academic Purposes course, and which can be transferred across contexts (specify the contexts).

2. On the 'specific' side, try to outline the aspects of the literacy employed by a discipline of which you are a member (e.g. what values, argument structures, vocabulary, grammar and genres are peculiar to this discipline).

1.4 Summary of the chapter

This chapter has discussed the defining features of ESP, noting its learner-centredness, its tendency to adopt methodologies from the discipline or occupation of the students, and its focus on the language (register and genre) – what students use in their studies or occupation. It has considered arguments in favour of specificity. These include the fact that 'general' English does not help the students very much with their academic studies or their job; also, their subject teachers will not or cannot teach them the specific language they need for their studies or job. Secondly, relying on the 'common core' of skills and language that are common to all academic disciplines is not possible, because different disciplines use language quite differently.

1.5 What should a teacher do after reading this chapter?

Identify a group of students – whether in academic studies or in an occupation – for whom you would like to design a specific purposes course. Describe what you know about the students, about their needs, about the language they use in their academic studies or their occupation. List what you don't know about the students, their needs and the specific language they use.

Chapter 2

Needs analysis in ESP

2.1 Introduction

This book is for English teachers of post-secondary students who are currently teaching English for Specific Purposes, or who are interested in moving to teaching English for Specific Purposes. It is also for high school English teachers whose students currently study one of their content subjects in English, or whose students will move into tertiary studies or employment where they will need to use English for a specific purpose.

The notion of 'specific purposes' is important. To gain the most benefit from the book, readers need to have in mind a specific purpose for which their students are learning English. This is easy for readers who are currently teaching English for Specific Purposes. You have a good idea what your students' specific English needs are. However, what if you are not currently teaching English for Specific Purposes, but are interested in moving to teaching English for Specific Purposes? Try to think of a specific purposes context that most interests you. Is it Business English? Medical English? Engineering English? English for a particular workplace? What if you are a secondary teacher whose students don't currently have needs for English for a specific purpose, but you want to prepare your students for tertiary studies or for a particular workplace? Here you might consult your students and ask them what courses they intend to study at tertiary level or what jobs they intend to do that need English.

Task 2.1

Write a few sentences to describe your students and their specific purpose. What is their discipline of study or their job? What are your students going to use English for? Where are they going to use English? Who will they use English with? What is their reason for using English? What makes the English they will use different from 'general' English?

2.2 Why do we need to analyse our students' language learning needs?

We are all aware of how the kind of language we use varies from context to context. With friends we are more informal than with strangers. Our academic writing and speaking are more formal than other writing and speaking we do. Our writing and speaking in the workplace are more 'business-like' than elsewhere. And of course, our language varies depending on our discipline of study or our workplace.

So, we can be sure that the language our learners need will also be specific to their intended context: the language learning needs of English for Specific Purposes students are specific by definition. Their needs are specific to their workplace or their area of study. As an ESP teacher, probably you have never worked in your students' workplace, or studied for the degree that they are studying. So how can you find out what those language learning needs are? Sometimes there are textbooks you can use. For example, Business English is a popular area of ESP, so you probably know of a Business English textbook. But how can you be sure that what is taught in that textbook is applicable to your students? Can the same Business English textbook be applicable to those in the workplace and those studying economics or accountancy? Other areas of ESP are new, and there is no available textbook. What can the teacher do? The answer is that teachers can investigate their students' language learning needs.

2.3 What is needs analysis?

In doing a needs analysis, the teacher investigates what their students need to use English for. Do they need to write in English? What do they need to write? Is it course assignments? What kind of assignments do they need to write? Is it business reports, or emails? Do they need to speak in English? Who do they need to speak to, and for what purpose? Do they need to speak on the phone, give talks or deal with customers? Do they need to read in English? If so, what do they need to read, and why?

Task 2.2

1. Think about your specific purposes context.
2. Write a few sentences to describe what you know about what your students use English for currently or what they'll use it for in the future.
3. Now write down what you feel you don't know about what your students use English for currently or what they'll use it for in the future.

2.3.1 What are needs?

Hutchinson and Waters (1987, pp.55-57) considered needs from three perspectives. These were necessities, lacks and wants:

a) The first perspective concerns the language requirements of the situation in which the learner needs to use English. Hutchinson and Waters called these **necessities**, which they described as 'the type of need determined by the demands of the target situation, that is, what the learner has to know in order to function effectively in the target situation'. Importantly, the teacher / needs analyst needs to find out: What tasks, activities and skills do the learners need to use English for? What should the learners ideally know and be able to do?

b) The second perspective concerns what the learner still needs to learn before they can function well in the situation in which they need to use English. Hutchinson and Waters called these **lacks**, describing these as 'what the learner knows already, so that you can decide which of the necessities the learner lacks. [...] The target proficiency [...] needs to be matched against the existing proficiency of the learners.' As an ESP teacher / needs analyst you would be interested in the proficiency level of the students, their language learning goals, and their age, interests, disciplinary specialization and/or (intended) workplace.

c) The third perspective concerns what the learners 'want or feel they need'. Hutchinson and Waters called these **wants**. As ESP teachers we need to take account of what the learners feel they need in order to give the course face value with the learners. If the learners feel the course is not fulfilling their needs, the course will be less effective.

d) A fourth consideration is the constraints of the **context** that you work in. What is the 'culture' of the institution that you work at (attitudes to innovation, teacher autonomy etc.)? How much freedom are you given to choose what you teach or how you implement the curriculum?

Task 2.3

Think of your chosen specific purposes context.

1. How could you find out about the 'necessities' or requirements of the situation in which the learner needs to use English?

2. How could you find out about learner 'lacks' or what the learners still need to learn before they can function well in the situation in which they need to use English?

3. How could you find out about what the learners want?

4. How does the institutional context influence what you teach?

2.3.2 Whose needs?

As ESP teachers, we are usually held accountable to the institution that we work at to teach our students the English that the institution feels the students need, or that will make things easier for the content teachers to teach. When students enter tertiary institutions or people enter workplaces, they are required to fit into the communicative practices of the tertiary institution or workplace. This serves the needs of the institution or workplace, but it might not necessarily serve the needs of the students or workers (Auerbach, 1995; Benesch, 2001).

Huhta et al (2013) say that ideally, we need to consider firstly individual learner needs, secondly the needs of the institution/workplace and thirdly the needs of the wider society. Huhta et al use the following workplace example to illustrate this:

> Needs of the individual learner: 'I need to be more confident with visitors.'
>
> Needs of the workplace: 'Our company needs to accommodate our business partners.'
>
> Needs of society: 'Our economy needs to have well-trained employees with good English skills because we rely on exports.'

Equally we could think of an example related to students in a tertiary context, such as engineering students:

> Needs of the individual learner: 'I need to be able to write case study assignments and give oral presentations.'
>
> Needs of the educational institution: 'We need students to have good language skills so that they can understand their textbooks, write their assignments well, and have good speaking skills for when they work in industry once they graduate.'
>
> Needs of society: 'For safety and economic reasons, it's important for our engineers to be able to communicate well with other engineers in our own country and in other countries.'

Task 2.4

Consider the learners in your specific purposes context.

1. What language needs do learners have in order to do well in their studies or job?

2. What needs does the institution/workplace have in relation to the learners?

3. What needs does society have in relation to the learners?

2.4 What methods can we use to do a needs analysis?

As we saw above, we need to take account of different perspectives on needs including the needs of individual learners, the institution/workplace and society. We also need to take account of Hutchinson and Waters' distinction between what is needed in the context (necessities), what the learner already knows or does not know (lacks) and what the learner wants. This makes it necessary to draw on several sources of information on learner needs. It is an important aspect of needs analysis often referred to as **triangulation**. Triangulation is the use of multiple methods or sources of information. It allows the needs analyst to develop an in-depth understanding, and greatly increases the validity of the findings.

Sample study 2.1   Triangulating of sources of information about learner needs

Cameron (1998) reports on an analysis of the language needs of EFL/ESL graduate students in a nursing programme in the School of Nursing at Pennsylvania, US. The participants had a range of first languages including Chinese, Japanese, Thai and Arabic. A diagnostic English speaking test was administered to incoming students. Those with a lower score were put into a general English programme. However, some were dissatisfied because the classes did not help them sufficiently perform specific tasks such as scientific research writing, communicating with ill children or recognising patterns of speech that indicate that a patient is in denial. Therefore, an ESP programme was created to respond to student language needs.

Data for the study was collected from several sources: (1) interviews with four senior staff members in the School of Nursing, (2) workshop observations, (3) student demographics, and (4) ethnographic observations and tape recordings in four different clinical sites. The study identified five categories of language needs students had, including (1) speech production accuracy (pronunciation, grammar, vocabulary and discourse), (2) academic performance (e.g. reading strategies, writing, speaking, critical thinking and moral reasoning), (3) clinical performance (e.g. getting information, transmitting information, translating information), (4) dialect (cultural) variation, and (5) inferencing skills. These categories may be useful for course designers of English for Nursing.

2.4.1 Who can teachers speak to in order to find out about learner needs?

So who are the people that we as teachers can consult in order to gain insights about learner needs? They include experts, students, and, in the workplace, customers or clients. Experts are probably the most reliable source of information. They have access to discipline-specific or workplace-specific language because they use that language themselves in their work. However, even experts can have faulty beliefs and intuitions about the language required. Experts can report on what they think is the right way to use language in their discipline or workplace, but the language that they actually use might be different. By studying what experts actually do in their own language use, we can get a more reliable picture. For example, many tertiary teachers tell their students never to use personal language like 'I' and 'we' in their writing. But researchers who study academic writing such as Hyland (2002a) and Harwood (2005) have shown that 'I' and 'we' are used in academic writing for a range of purposes. In Parkinson (2020) I compare the use of these pronouns in the writing of novice L2 writers with that of more expert students.

We can also consult learners about their needs. Of course such consultation is important, because it allows us to find out what learners would prefer: their 'wants' in Hutchinson and Waters' (1987) terms. Learners can also tell us what they find difficult, or their experience of using discipline-specific or workplace-specific language, which can guide the teacher about what to focus on in teaching. But tertiary students' knowledge of their disciplinary language needs is usually limited, because their experience of this language is limited. Learners who already have experience of the workplace may be more knowledgeable.

Task 2.5

> Which experts could you interview in order to gain insights into the demands your learners will face in the target situation? Develop a set of interview prompts that you could use to interview one of these experts (Basturkmen 2010, p.34).

2.4.2 Methods of collecting data about learner needs

In addition to our considering who we can consult about learner needs, there are a number of methods we can use to gather this information. An important and very useful method is interviews, either with experts or with students. Interviews provide in-depth knowledge and understanding, where the interviewer can probe beyond the questions they thought of, and thus discover things they have not considered before. However, interviewing requires skills; the interviewer must be careful not to influence the interviewees.

Using interviews to gain information about learner needs

Spence and Liu (2013) studied the language needs of process integration engineers in the technology industry in Taiwan, China. Data collection was carried out at a semiconductor manufacturing company. A questionnaire was used to survey 121 engineers, and 11 engineers participated in interviews. The questionnaire and interviews were then triangulated with interviews for customers. Findings were that writing and reading were used more often than listening and speaking, and that listening and speaking were the most difficult for the engineers, particularly when they were communicating with foreign customers. In the workplace, reading and writing were used most frequently for emails, whilst speaking and listening were used most often at company meetings. Building relationships with foreign customers was a general requirement. The needs and challenges raised by the engineers aligned with the customers' perception that engineers in this context had difficulty in speaking and listening. This study suggests that English courses for engineers should include instruction in email writing, together with speaking and listening skills for teleconferencing.

Surveys and questionnaires can also be useful. They enable a larger number of people to be consulted. An advantage is that they are standardised so there is less chance of the interviewer influencing the answers; in addition, a lot of data can be collected. However, because the teachers and researchers doing the needs analysis are unaware of what they don't know, they may neglect to ask about important aspects.

Sample study 2.3   Using questionnaires to gain information about learner needs

Chan (2014) investigated the communicative needs of business professionals in order to develop more effective Business English courses. The context was Hong Kong, China workplaces. A questionnaire survey which was completed by two hundred and fifteen experienced business professionals working in a wide range of professions was used to collect data. The study sought to understand professionals' spoken and written needs in their workplace, the challenges they encountered, what aspects of spoken and written communication were the most difficult for them, and their concerns about current Business English course content. Chan found that telephoning, and informal meetings and discussions were the most common spoken communication, and that internal emails were the most common written communication. The participants experienced business plans, business publicity, contracts and business proposals as the most difficult types of written communication. Press briefings and business negotiations were experienced as the most challenging spoken communication. Overall, the participants thought current Business English courses were not strongly relevant to workplace communication. They expressed several concerns including irrelevance of the course content, overemphasis on the academic aspects and failure to meet communicative needs in the workplace.

One implication for English for Business courses and coursebooks was that topics that are important for spoken and written communication, i.e. emails, reports, telephoning, meetings/discussions, should be covered. In addition, the participants suggested that real-life cases should be used. Participants of this study said that their coursebooks did not meet the needs they encountered in the workplace. They also said that the coursebooks focused on academic aspects of language; they wanted informal aspects of language, but these were lacking in coursebooks.

Another very important method is observation. Imagine if you need to teach learners who are training to work in a shop. A good source of information would be observing retail employees and noting down the language they use with customers. Similarly, if your learners are training to work in tourism, to become receptionists in a hotel, then sitting in a hotel lobby and noting down the language that experienced receptionists use with those checking in or checking out would be useful. In the tertiary sector observing the contexts in which students must use language, such as lectures, workshops and laboratory sessions, would help the analyst identify the language that students need to learn.

(Sample study 2.4) Using observation to gain information about learner needs

Lu (2018) studied nurses in a large modern hospital in Taiwan, China, which is located in a modern city where a large number of foreigners live and work. The nurses therefore needed to be able to communicate with foreign patients, who were likely not to be proficient in Chinese. The hospital has a special centre to provide English-language medical services to foreign patients. Nine nurses were interviewed; the interviewees had three years of nursing experience, so they knew about the nature of hospital work. Ten surgical nurses were observed during the day shifts. Their work experience ranged from a few months to several years. Lu shadowed one nurse for all of her nursing duties for three days, then spent another day observing how the other nurses performed their jobs.

Interestingly, Lu found that the nurses used specialist language for communication with medical staff, but non-specialist language for communication with foreign patients. So the nurses needed not only the specialist technical vocabulary, but also the vocabulary that ordinary patients with no medical training could understand. Challenges experienced by the nurses included the unfamiliar accents of their patients, which they found difficult to understand. The nurses' pronunciation was also difficult for the patients to understand. Lu concluded that teaching to support the building of nurse–patient relationships as well as the development of communication competence would be useful.

Task 2.6

What observations could you make which would provide information about the language needs of your learners?

Another key method to find out learners' language needs is textual analysis. Teachers and analysts can analyse good examples of students' written texts, or recordings or transcriptions of spoken events such as lectures and student presentations. This is extremely valuable in showing what successful students do. However, textual analysis doesn't take contextual factors into account. Aspects like why the text was written in a certain way and what help was received from instructors are missing. Similarly, for transcriptions of spoken events, tone of voice, emphasis and aspects like laughter are also missing, which could make the analyst misinterpret the meaning. To get insights into context, observation and interviews are more useful.

Sample study 2.5

Parkinson (2017a) studied science student laboratory reports. I selected 60 laboratory reports from four different science disciplines (biology, food science, chemistry and engineering) that had received high grades. I sourced these laboratory reports from the British Academic Written English Corpus, which is a set of high-graded assignments from three British universities. My purpose was to find out firstly how successful students structure their writing of laboratory reports and secondly the language features of their writing. Parkinson (2017b) describes how to teach students to write a laboratory report using this move analysis.

Other methods used by needs analysts include tests (Jordan, 1997; Long, 2005) to get a sense of learners' 'lacks'. We saw in Sample study 2.1 above that Cameron (1998) used a diagnostic test of speaking in English as an initial step to assess incoming learners' current abilities. Learners can also be asked to assess themselves (Jordan, 1997). A study by Bacha and Bahous (2008) of business students' writing needs showed that students evaluated their writing level higher than the academic teaching staff did. Students and faculty had different understandings of writing needs and students reported a higher writing workload on all writing tasks. This gives valuable insights into how learners' experience of language tasks can be different from what their teachers anticipate. Both Long (2005) and Jordan (1997) also mention journals and logs, where learners keep a diary of their language-related activities. These also provide valuable in-depth information about learners' experience of and feelings about the language learning process. As we have seen in the sample studies above, another extremely important source of information is published research.

2.5 Summary of the chapter

This chapter has discussed how teachers can find out what the language needs of their students are, even when they themselves are not experts in the disciplinary area or workplace of their students. It has considered first of all what language learning needs the learner has. Following Hutchinson and Waters (1987), these were considered firstly from the perspective of what the learner needs in order to function well in the discipline or workplace ('necessities'). Secondly the learners' needs were considered from the point of view of what language the learner has already known and what they still need to learn ('lacks'). The learners' 'wants' were also considered. We noted that besides the learners' needs, the teacher also needs to consider the needs of the institution or workplace as well as the needs of society.

Next, we considered the people we can consult, who could inform us about the language the learners need to know. These include experts, the learners themselves and also the learners' potential clients or customers. Finally, the methods that teachers can use to find out learners' language needs were discussed, including interviews, questionnaires, observation, textual analysis, diagnostic tests, journals and finally, consulting published research.

2.6 What should a teacher do after reading this chapter?

As a teacher, after reading this chapter, you should make a written plan to analyse the needs of the learners that you are teaching or plan to teach. Who would you consult about your learners' language needs? Consider the needs analysis methods that are explained in this chapter (interviews, questionnaires, observation, textual analysis, tests, student self-assessment, student journals and logs, and reading published research). Which of these methods would you use to investigate the specific purposes situation that is of interest to you? Try to think of three or more methods that you could use, noting how they function to triangulate your findings.

Chapter 3

Qualitative approaches to investigating student needs

┌─ **Pre-reading questions** ─────────────────────┐

Before you start reading this chapter, think about the
following:
1) What different methods of finding out about students'
   language needs can you remember from Chapter 2?
2) What are qualitative research methods?
3) What are quantitative methods?
4) What are the main differences between them?
└───┘

3.1 Introduction

To investigate student needs, qualitative methods are very useful. These include interviews, observation, diaries and narratives. Qualitative methods are also the easiest for teachers to use, as they can be as simple as talking to colleagues who teach content subjects, or observing lectures or laboratory sessions in our students' content subjects. The focus of this chapter is qualitative methods that teachers can use to find out what their students' language needs are.

Qualitative methods involve the teacher in collecting information using a range of methods including interviews, observation, focus groups and diaries. The teacher would usually use more than one source of information, such as interviewing experts, observing class and holding focus group interviews with students. In addition, the teacher might analyse student assignments to see the kind of writing or speaking the students need to do. This gives the teacher a more in-depth and reliable picture of the students' needs than using a single method would do. It allows the teacher to develop an interpretive and explanatory account of what people in a particular discipline or workplace do. The aim is for the teacher to gain insights not only into what people do, but also why they do it, what they aim to achieve and what it means to them. It helps if the teacher/investigator looks at the workplace as having a particular 'culture', with particular values and ways of doing things. For example, as teachers we are familiar with the 'culture' of the school setting – how we do things, and what our values are, like what we view as good teaching, and what we and our colleagues accept as normal. We expect the culture of the school setting to be quite different from a building site for example, or a corporate environment.

3.2 Some examples of studies of ESP students' language needs using qualitative methods

We now look at some examples of how qualitative methods have been used to investigate ESP students' needs. We will look firstly at two examples of the language needs of students in full-time education, and then two examples of language needs in the workplace.

3.2.1 Using qualitative methods to investigate language needs at university: science students

I'm going to start by looking at my own experience of using qualitative methods to investigate my ESP students' language learning needs. This relates to my experience as an ESP teacher of science students. The students were first-year chemistry students at a South African university. In this context, the social and political contexts were important, as South Africa is a very unequal society, and my ESP students, who were from rural backgrounds, had attended schools which were not well-resourced.

The context of my investigation was the chemistry laboratory. I chose the laboratory because laboratory sessions are central to undergraduate science. In the laboratory, students learn the laboratory methods, skills and problem-solving which are essential to professional scientists. They learn the values of science, including the idea that objects and phenomena can be investigated through measurement. Students learn to talk about science with their laboratory partners, to read about science in their laboratory manuals and to write about science in their laboratory reports. Those who learn the skills necessary to work in a laboratory can later seek work in laboratories or progress to graduate research. The laboratory session is therefore a 'gatekeeping' event that determines access to occupational and educational opportunities (Michaels, 1981).

I planned to observe students' learning ways of talking and writing about science. My students, all L2 speakers of English, were studying alongside L1 English speakers. Both L2 and L1 speakers were acquiring the specialised language needed for studying chemistry. I collected a number of different kinds of data, including observation and field notes; audio recordings of participants in the laboratory; interviews with students and staff; textual analysis of the laboratory manual; and textual analysis of student reports.

I now share some recordings I made during the laboratory session. Figure 3.1 shows an extract from the pre-laboratory lecture given by Dr Stevens, who was the staff member in charge of the laboratory session. [Please note that following extracts and interview quotations in this book may have been transcribed word for word, which means that grammatical errors are not corrected.]

| Figure 3.1 | Dr Stevens' lecture at the start of a laboratory session |

> **Dr Stevens:** Now you're going to be working as a group per bench, alright, so it's <u>a case of division of labour</u>; everyone's got to do their little bit, um, work as a group and sort it out amongst yourselves. You paying attention chaps? OK. make sure you are please. So work as group, <u>chop up the, um, procedures and the bits and pieces within each and make sure you've got no passengers</u>, OK. Alright, so all your results are going to be common, so you all get it right and you'll get the marks for it.

Task 3.1

Look at the underlined parts of Dr Stevens' statement in Figure 3.1. From what he says here, what is more important to Dr Stevens? Conceptual understanding, problem-solving or efficiency?

In Figure 3.2 I share an extract of three students interacting at the laboratory bench. The three students were: Helen, a female student for whom English was a first language; Bongi, a female student for whom English was a second language; Nkosinathi, a male student for whom English was a second language. We can see that the focus of the students is on interpreting the meaning of their laboratory manual and achieving what it instructs them to do.

Figure 3.2 Student interaction during a laboratory session

Helen:	Hurry up and take it out to see if it's partially frozen.
Bongi:	Isn't it frozen?
Helen:	Can you see if it's partially frozen?
Nkosinathi:	It's freezing down there.
Helen:	You mustn't let it freeze too much, hey.
Bongi:	Yes, it must be partially frozen.
Helen:	OK, (quotes from the manual) 'Hold the test tube in the bath until the solvent partially freezes'. OK. Do you think it's partially yet? Do you think that's partially frozen?

The third extract, in Figure 3.3, is from an interview with Dr Stevens. Dr Stevens' focus for the laboratory session is on students doing the tasks as instructed in the laboratory manual. It is not on the students' discussion of concepts or them working out what to do by discussion.

Figure 3.3 Interview with academic staff member, Dr Stevens

Dr Stevens:	They've got 3 hours to get it done. It stops them sitting around chattering.
Interviewer:	Is student talk during the lab important?
Dr Stevens:	No. They don't need to talk to each other; in fact, it irritates me so much. You can watch and they'll get distracted, start talking and their hands will slow down, and they'll stop. Or they drop something, or they break something, or they set themselves on fire.

We can see from Figure 3.1, Figure 3.2 and Figure 3.3 that the three data sources (two observations and one interview) supported each other. All three of them suggest that learning to do the activities in the laboratory manual is treated as the most important objective of the laboratory. Understanding concepts and solving problems are less of an expectation. Thus, the advantage of using qualitative methods is that it allowed me as the ESP teacher and researcher to take an in-depth look at the language needs of students in laboratory sessions from multiple perspectives. These perspectives supported each other and added validity to the interpretation. Another advantage is that these methods allowed me an insider perspective, as I was a non-participant observer in the laboratory session.

Another qualitative method is textual analysis. In Figure 3.4, I include an extract from the laboratory manual. I have shown the verbs in italicised bold.

Figure 3.4 Extract from the laboratory manual

'*Fit* the test tube with its thermometer and stirrer and *place* it into a cooling mixture that *should contain* several pieces of ice at all times. *Use* enough cooling liquid to cover the level of the solvent in the test tube. The bath *should be stirred* frequently to ensure a uniform temperature throughout.'

Task 3.2

1. Look carefully at the verbs in italicised bold in Figure 3.4. Are these declaratives, interrogatives or imperatives?

2. What does this suggest about the purpose of the laboratory manual?

3. According to the laboratory manual, what is the main purpose of the laboratory – doing actions, or understanding concepts and solving problems?

The disadvantage of using qualitative methods in this project is the concern that the analysis relies on the researcher's interpretation. Most people find it difficult to recognise and correct for their own bias. However, using multiple data sources (observation, interview and textual analysis) corrects for this to an extent. A second disadvantage is what is known as the **observer paradox**: To what extent do observing and studying the event change the participants' behaviour? Maybe the participants wanted to please me by giving me the answers they thought I wanted.

3.2.2 Using qualitative methods to investigate language needs at university: MBA students

As in the above example from my experience of teaching science students, a study by Northcott (2001) also involves university students. Northcott describes the qualitative investigation she undertook when she was designing an ESP course for MBA students who were speakers of English as a second or foreign language. She wanted to know what their language needs were in order for them to participate in an MBA programme at the University of Edinburgh. As in my example of science laboratories above, Northcott focuses on a particular event, and one that was important to the students' course of study. This event was the interactive lectures in the MBA. Northcott was interested in the students' understanding of these interactive lectures and ability to participate orally in them. The interactive lectures involved 20 or more students led by a lecturer. Subject input was provided by the lecturer, but the students needed to participate orally in a variety of ways. Northcott's methods included observation, interviews with lecturers and students, and questionnaires.

Northcott reports that some of the aspects that were difficult for the students were the result of differences between these interactive lectures and regular lectures where students were not expected to participate orally. The students were not entirely sure about the status of other students' contributions. When other students put forward viewpoints that were different from that of the lecturer, it could be confusing to decide what the correct answer was. The fact that the lecturer stated that there may be other viewpoints than her own added to this confusion. Other cultural difficulties were references to local politics, and the use of humour and irony, which is more difficult to interpret in a second language. Northcott concluded that the students found it helpful when the lecturer made links between the lectures and the textbook, and between current and previous material. They also found it helpful when the lecturer rephrased and summarised students' answers. The students were graduates with business experience from around the world, so their sharing of their expertise in presentations was also helpful.

Northcott's methods of recording parts of the lectures, observing lectures, and interviews allowed for an in-depth understanding of the requirements of taking part in the interactive lectures.

They allowed her to assess what was difficult for the students, and where her ESP course could support the students' language needs.

Task 3.3

> Think of the ESP students you teach or that you would like to teach. What do you think you might learn from attending and observing one of their content classes?

3.2.3 Using qualitative methods to investigate language needs in the workplace: auditors

The above examples show how ESP teachers working at university, college or school can investigate their students' specific language learning needs. However, teachers involved in teaching ESP to those in the workplace or about to enter the workplace can use similar methods. We find this in the following study undertaken by Flowerdew and Wan (2010). The authors were interested in the language needs of students in Hong Kong, China who were training to be financial auditors and tax accountants. One of their language needs was the writing of audit reports. The authors used genre analysis to identify the organisation and linguistic features of the audit report. They found that the audit report consisted of the sections found in Table 3.1.

Table 3.1 The audit report (Flowerdew & Wan, 2010)

Parts of the audit report	Purpose of this part
Summary of credible actions taken	Tells the readers that the financial statements were audited

(to be continued)

(*continued*)

Parts of the audit report	Purpose of this part
Address responsibilities	Reports the responsibilities of the directors of the client company and the responsibilities of the auditors
Opinion	Mentions the method of the audit and, if appropriate, expresses positive evaluation of the financial statements
Emphasis of matters	The auditors draw the readers' attention to any problem in the financial statements
Qualified opinion	Rarely, when the financial statements largely comply with regulations, but the auditors are unable to confirm certain things, they might make a qualified opinion
Disclaimer of opinion	Very rarely, when there is a serious problem with the financial statements, the auditors note that the financial statements cannot be relied upon

But the authors realised that this text-based analysis was not enough. They wanted to know about why the audit report is organised as it is, how it is produced, which parts are written following a template, and which parts vary more between audit reports. They wanted to know how the auditors reach their conclusions. To gain insights about this, the authors used observation of the auditing process by professional auditors in their workplace, as well as in-depth interviews, and verification of their analysis, which was checked by a professional auditor.

The auditors doing their work were observed by the researchers on three occasions, including an initial three-hour session at their company offices, a three-hour session at the client company and a final three-hour session back at the auditors' offices. They observed how the work of the audit was divided amongst the team. The researchers noticed the use of several languages amongst the team: Mandarin, Cantonese and English. They found that there was a need for oral proficiency in all three languages and a need for written proficiency in English. The auditors shifted between languages, depending on whom they were speaking to. While speaking Mandarin and Cantonese, they also used English technical terms such as *open market value*, *assets* and *depreciate*. The researchers noted the importance of group discussion during the audit, and joint problem-solving by the auditors. They also noted the range of modes of communication including texting, telephoning, emails and face-to-face communication.

The researchers also conducted reflective in-depth interviews with four auditors and a technical manager. This gave them insights into how the auditors wrote their audit report, the extent to which they relied on templates and the role of the technical manager, especially when the client's accounts had been assessed to be problematic by the auditors or when complex ideas needed to be expressed. These methods of observation and interviews were very useful as they gave the researchers insights into how standardised and formulaic the audit report is. Auditors have access to templates and prior reports, so they are able to draw on them when drafting their reports. Nevertheless, when reports draw attention to problems and irregularities in the client's accounts, there is a need for original writing.

(Task 3.4)

> What do you find most interesting or surprising about what Flowerdew and Wan's study discovered about the language needs of auditors?

Flowerdew and Wan used the qualitative methods of observation and interviews, and the text-based method of genre analysis to investigate their students' language needs in future workplace. The use of several different methods to provide different perspectives on the same thing is mentioned above as 'triangulation'. We can think of the different corners of a triangle as different perspectives (for example, the perspective from observation and the perspective from interviews). The third corner of the triangle would be the observed event in which language is being used (such as the laboratory, the participative lectures and the auditors' offices described above).

3.2.4 Using qualitative methods to investigate language needs in the workplace: nurses

As a second example focusing on students' language needs in the workplace, I will now look at a study by Bosher and Stocker (2015) of why and how nurses in the EFL context of Taiwan, China used English in their workplace, the hospital. Participants were 19 full-time students in a master's programme. They were all women in their late 20's to late 30's whose L1 was Chinese.

Their English proficiency level was B1. They used English to communicate with doctors and other health-care professionals. They also needed to communicate with foreign caregivers about patient care, as well as with foreign patients. A different qualitative approach was used compared with those described above. In Bosher and Stocker's study, the participants provided written narratives on their use of English in the hospital. Although this was the only qualitative method they used, as we will see below, the nurses' narratives provided very useful and in-depth information about language needs of the nurses in the programme.

Bosher and Stocker found that the reasons that the nurses reported for using English included improving the quality of nursing care, professionalism, and career advancement. English was used for multiple purposes, some of which included asking for information, giving instructions, explaining, responding to questions, informing, and engaging in small talk. Reading what doctors had written in English and reading up-to-date literature in English were also mentioned. Nurses reported documenting patient care in English. One nurse noted that in some hospitals, 'we must writing individual nursing plan and note [in English]' (Bosher & Stocker 2015, p.114).

Communicating with foreign patients was another reason that nurses mentioned for what they needed to do in English. One reported that 'last year I met a foreign laborer who had a head injury, he had been transferred from the Emergency Room to the Intensive Care Unit. He asked, "Where is here?" "Who are you?" and "Why do you put so many strange things on my body?" It took him a long time to [accept] being on my floor' (Bosher & Stocker 2015, p.114).

Communicating with foreign caregivers was also mentioned. One nurse reported that 'I said, "How long have you cared for the patient at home?" [The foreign caregiver] said to me, "I have cared for the patient for three years. I do not know his condition is critical and need to insert endotracheal tube." I said, "Don't worry! The patient is on critical stage now. But we make effort to care him. And I can teach you how to care [for] the patient" (Bosher & Stocker 2015, p.114).

Overall, this study showed that using English at work amongst nurses ran in parallel with the increasing use of English in Taiwan, China as the region aimed at internationalisation.

(Task 3.5)

Consider the ESP course that you are currently teaching or would like to teach.

1. Make a plan of how you could use qualitative methods to investigate the language needs of this group.

2. How many methods would you use?

3. What written or spoken text or event would you focus on?

4. Why have you selected this text or event?

5. What observations would you make in the learners' content subject or workplace?

6. Who would you interview and why?

7. Would you do any textual analysis? If yes, what would you analyse?

8. Would you include any other sources of information?

In addition to qualitative methods, ESP teachers also use text-based analysis, which refers to methods where we focus on and analyse spoken or written texts that students need either for their studies or in the workplace. These text-based methods will be the subject of later chapters, including Chapter 6 (genre analysis) and Chapter 7 (register analysis).

3.3 Summary of the chapter

Qualitative methods allow ESP teachers to gain an in-depth understanding of their ESP students' language needs. These methods include interviews, observation, focus groups, diaries and narratives. Use of more than one qualitative method is useful because it allows teachers to get more than one perspective on the language that their ESP students need to use. Qualitative methods can give us valuable information about the language needs of students, whether at university, college or school. They can also provide insights into the language needs of those in the workplace. Qualitative methods can be used in conjunction with text-based methods or quantitative methods.

3.4 What should a teacher do after reading this chapter?

Think about the qualitative methods discussed in this chapter and name as many of them as you can. What advantages and disadvantages do you see in each of these methods? Which methods would it be possible for you to use in investigating your students' specific purposes needs?

Implement the plan of using qualitative methods to investigate your ESP students' language needs, which you made in Task 3.5. If possible, collaborate with a colleague. Each of you can gather information using a different method. Meet with your colleague to identify where the information gathered by the use of each method is in agreement and where it does not agree.

Chapter 4

Curriculum development in ESP

Pre-reading questions

Before you start reading this chapter, think about the following:

1) What is a curriculum?

2) What things do you think are important to consider when a curriculum is being developed?

4.1 Introduction

A curriculum provides a guide for teachers of what the goals of the teaching are. It involves the instruction that learners get during their education, and the planning, teaching and evaluation of the instruction. It includes the planned content, materials, and experiences that provide students with information, practice and proficiency. Language curricula vary according to the assumptions of curriculum developers about language, language learning, teacher and learner roles, effective learning activities, and preferred instructional materials (Christison & Murray, 2021). So when we design or use a curriculum we need to be aware of what our own assumptions about these things are.

Because ESP courses often respond to specific local needs, it is sometimes the role of the teacher to develop the curriculum. Where a curriculum is available, it may still need to be developed further because student demographics may change, or the needs of the students' discipline may change. Curricula should not be viewed as unchanging and unchangeable. They need to be responsive to the students' needs. It is therefore important for ESP teachers to have knowledge of the process of curriculum development.

A general model of curriculum development is usually stated as planning > implementing > evaluating. However, the process is not really linear, starting with planning, moving through implementing and ending with evaluating the curriculum. Instead, it is recursive, meaning that we start by planning but when we move to implementation, we realise that the plan needs adjustment, so we return to the planning stage before proceeding to implementation again. Then when we reach the evaluation stage, we might realise that something is missing, so we need to go back, and adjust the plan and implement the curriculum again. Thus, curriculum development involves a back-and-forth process, gradually being adjusted towards a curriculum that's appropriate for the students.

As noted above, the curriculum is a guide for teachers concerning what the goals of the teaching are. The goals are important, because, like travellers, we need to know our destination before we start our journey. Wiggins and McTighe (2005) talked about 'backwards design'. As shown in Figure 4.1, this means starting with our goals for teaching (knowing what we want the students to know by the end of the course) and working backwards from the goals and to the development of assessment tasks and then teaching and learning activities.

| Figure 4.1 | Backwards design |

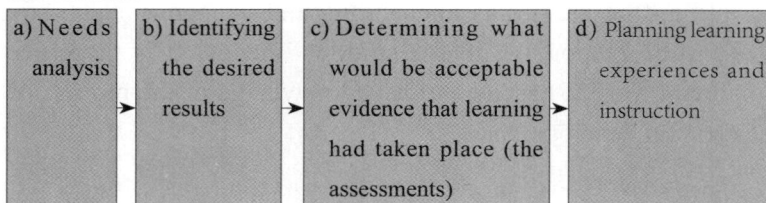

a) Needs analysis	b) Identifying the desired results	c) Determining what would be acceptable evidence that learning had taken place (the assessments)	d) Planning learning experiences and instruction

4.2 Developing the curriculum

In developing a curriculum, Christison and Murray (2021) suggest that there are three stages. These are: understanding the context in which the language learning is taking place; developing curriculum relevant to the context; and evaluating the curriculum.

4.2.1 Understanding the context

To understand the context, it is important to consider the sociocultural context, referring to the fact that the culture and society in which the language is used will have a big influence on the way that language is used and taught. By culture and society, we include the larger culture and society, the culture of the institution at which the learning takes place and the culture of the students' discipline of study, or of the students' workplace. What beliefs and practices related to language learning and teaching are prevalent in the broader culture, in the institution and in the discipline or workplace? What outcomes are expected of learners?

To plan the curriculum, it is important to take account of the stakeholders' needs and the learners' needs. We have considered how to investigate these needs in Chapter 2. Curriculum planning also requires us to consider the institution at which the curriculum will be taught, and the disciplinary department or workplace. We should also think about what the learners have already known and what they can already do, as well as what they need to know or be able to do.

Task 4.1

Think and write down your ideas about the following questions:

1. In your experience, what beliefs and practices related to language learning and teaching are prevalent in the larger culture and society you are in?

2. What beliefs and practices related to language learning are prevalent in the institution that you teach at?

3. What beliefs and practices related to language learning are prevalent in the discipline of the students that you teach or plan to teach in (e.g. business, nursing etc.)?

Sample study 4.1   **Planning a curriculum for a workplace course in a Japanese company**

Cowling (2007) reports on his planning of a curriculum for a large Japanese company. He was asked to develop a course that would enable students to adapt their knowledge of general English to the business situations they were exposed to in their jobs. The students were pre-service employees, who had little knowledge of the language needs of their future jobs. Cowling consulted several people and groups about what the students' language needs were. The most useful group were senior staff members who had good insights into the context as they were already doing the jobs. Cowling used a questionnaire for the pre-service employees to complete with their experienced colleagues. They reported needs as being:

- Understanding cultural differences between the employees and their business partners
- Undertaking negotiations with business partners; meetings, placing orders, and telephone conversations

- Describing business trends
- Introductions and greetings, hosting business visitors, and general small talk

Based on this information, Cowling designed a syllabus that drew on a notional-functional approach which took account of the functions such as business introductions, hosting visitors, business telephoning, placing orders, and describing business trends that the employees would have to perform in their jobs. His syllabus was also based in the content of the employees' future jobs. This involved describing products and services, business presentations, business meetings and business negotiations.

4.2.2 Developing curriculum relevant to the context

One of the first things to do when we develop a curriculum is to consider what the intended goals and objectives of the curriculum are. What do we want the learners to be able to do once they have finished the course? Goals refer to the broad long-term intentions of teaching. They are written from the teacher's point of view. Each goal has several related objectives, which are narrower, more specific and which successful students will achieve during the course. Learning objectives refer to specific language that the learners will know or specific language-related abilities that the learners will achieve by the end of the course. The use of needs analysis is essential in deciding what the goals and objectives of the course should be.

Table 4.1 Examples of goals and objectives in English for Specific Purposes

Context of learning	Goals	Related learning objectives
Business professionals employed in a company that does business internationally	To develop spoken English language competency for professional purposes for interacting with clients	By the end of the course: • Students will be able to <u>take</u> telephone messages • Students will be able to <u>greet</u> visitors • Students will be able to <u>interact with</u> clients in business meetings
University students studying engineering	To develop writing abilities for engineering studies	By the end of the course: • Students will be able to <u>use</u> appropriate organisation, vocabulary and style in writing engineering case studies • Students will be able to <u>draw on</u> literature appropriately in writing engineering assignments

Objectives must have an observable, measurable action or capability. These are underlined in Table 4.1. Words like 'understand' should not be used, because it is not possible to measure understanding. Instead we would use words like 'explain' or 'summarise' to express this meaning. The following are examples of the kinds of actions and capabilities objectives can refer to (Bloom, 1956):

Table 4.2 Verbs for writing learning objectives: observable, measurable actions or capabilities

Knowledge	Understand	Apply	Analyse	Evaluate	Create
Define	Explain	Apply	Analyse	Criticise	Design
Identify	Describe	Illustrate	Compare	Evaluate	Compose
Describe	Interpret	Modify	Classify	Order	Create
Label	Paraphrase	Use	Contrast	Recommend	Plan
List	Summarise	Change	Distinguish	Compare	Combine
Name	Classify	Choose	Infer	Summarise	Formulate
State	Compare	Demonstrate	Categorise	Support	Hypothesise

Task 4.2

Consider the ESP students that you teach or intend to teach.

1. Write one teacher goal for a course for these students.
2. Write two learner objectives related to this teacher goal.

Also important in developing a curriculum is what the approach to teaching will be. Approaches that are appropriate to English for Specific Purposes include a theme-based approach, a genre-based approach, an academic language functions approach, a notional-functional approach etc. We consider appropriate approaches to curriculum design in Chapter 5.

Another question relates to the language content that learners need to learn in order to achieve the goals of the curriculum, and how this content should be organised. A typical focus is the genres that learners need for their discipline of study or their workplace. We will focus on genre in Chapter 6. Another typical focus is register, meaning the linguistic features of the language used by a particular group of people (e.g. by medical professionals, or by lawyers or teachers). The language they use will have a specific range of language features (including level of formality) that are frequent in that particular discipline or workplace. For example, typical language of teachers in the classroom includes interrogatives and imperatives. Chapter 7 focuses on register. Yet another typical focus is speech acts and speech functions. For example, the speech acts that are essential in a retail workplace are greeting the customers, offering the customers help, suggesting items for sale, taking payment etc. In New Zealand, an important speech act for retail workers is making small talk (e.g. 'Nice weather we're having'). A course for retail workers could be organised around learning these speech functions. A course for learners who will need to interact with people from a foreign culture in their workplace might benefit from content related to sociocultural appropriacy. For example, how formal or informal do they expect their business partners to be? How is (in)formality achieved in the language that will be used? What expectations do the business partners have in relation to expression of power differences? What topics should be avoided with people of the foreign culture because they consider these topics to be inappropriate to talk about? Etc.

Selecting learning materials and activities for the curriculum involves considering the materials that will help learners deal with the language in their discipline or workplace, acquire the content with the language in their discipline or workplace, and achieve the course objectives. Materials need to be appropriate to achieve curriculum objectives. In Chapter 8 we will consider materials development. Another consideration is how learning will be assessed. Like teaching approaches and materials, assessment must be appropriate to the curriculum objectives. In ESP courses for workplaces, assessment might involve assessment of a workplace task. For example, for a course for retail workers mentioned above, assessment might involve assessing learners' ability to interact with a customer. We will consider assessment in ESP in Chapter 9.

As discussed above, the goals and objectives are a starting point of the curriculum development process. When we come to implement the curriculum, each lesson must also have an objective that is linked to one of the course objectives. When we design a lesson, it is good to start with this lesson objective, so that we have this objective in mind when we select and sequence the content of the lesson, develop the learning tasks, and assess students' learning.

4.2.3 Evaluating the curriculum

To evaluate the curriculum, we would evaluate whether instruction takes account of the values of the sociocultural context, and what impact the curriculum has on instruction. We would also assess whether student learning achieves the objectives of the curriculum, and whether their learning meets stakeholders' and students' needs. Evaluation of the curriculum can lead to revision, which is a return to the planning and implementation stages.

> **Sample study 4.2** Evaluating and revising a curriculum for a work-integrated learning module
>
> Chan (2021) reports on a process of evaluation-redesign-evaluation of a work-integrated learning (WIL) course for students at a university in Hong Kong, China. Firstly, Chan evaluated the existing module. Her methods included examining the existing curriculum documents, reading prior students' reflective reports and discussing informally with previous students. The problems that she identified were: students had unrealistic expectations of learning in the workplace; the module did not suggest what students could do to learn more in their workplace placements; the module did not encourage application of disciplinary knowledge to their work; students did not interact with each other while doing the module; students were not given guidance in reflecting on their work experience; a reflective report was written at the end of the work experience, but this did not help students improve during that experience. A new module was then designed to address these six problems.

In redesigning the module Chan incorporated needs analysis. Interviews with students who had taken the old module and with departmental staff who did WIL-related administrative work were also done. Ultimately, the goal of the new module was to help students discover their workplace communication needs. Once the curriculum had been redesigned, and had been in operation for a year, Chan evaluated the new module. Her sources of information for the evaluation were the course reflections of 46 students and a questionnaire survey after they had completed the module. These data sources showed that it was effective in helping the students learn proactively and in enabling them to identify key aspects of workplace communication, including their target situation, workplace discourse, their current language skills and lacks, and effective ways of learning workplace communication.

In addition to the methods used by Chan in Sample study 4.2, Christison and Murray (2021) suggest the following ways that we can evaluate the quality of the curriculum:
- classroom observation
- teacher input, such as offering suggestions or posing questions
- studies of student language samples and student test results
- action research

Task 4.3

Consider the ESP course that you are currently teaching and think about the curriculum evaluation methods above suggested by Chan (2021) and Christison and Murray (2021).
1. How could observing classroom interaction help you evaluate the curriculum?
2. Write down two questions to elicit teachers' opinions and

experience of the curriculum.

3. How would you use student language samples and student test results to evaluate the curriculum?

4.3 Teacher professional development

Most ESP teachers were originally trained as English language teachers. They have experience teaching English language, but little knowledge or experience of teaching language for a specific purpose. Because of this, it is valuable for teachers to receive professional development in ESP. A 2019 study by Bocanegra-Valle and Basturkmen, involving interviews with 19 experienced ESP teachers, found that the ESP teachers perceived themselves as needing professional development in the areas of 'course development, knowledge of the target discipline, knowledge of language use in the target discipline, peer collaboration, and professional development opportunities'.

Basturkmen (2014) notes the limited attention paid to the topic of ESP teacher education. Reviewing the studies that had been done on ESP teacher education so far, she included a number of strands: the role of specialised knowledge, the importance of culture and context knowledge in ESP teacher education, and strategies for compensating for gaps in subject knowledge.

ESP teachers with no or limited opportunities for professional development can work through books such as this one together with peers to develop their own expertise in ESP. In Section 4.1 we talked about 'backwards design' (Wiggins & McTighe, 2005). If you imagine yourself as a language teacher who is enrolled in a course on how to teach English for Specific Purposes, what would backwards design in that course involve? What would the learning objectives be? How would we assess whether those learning objectives had been achieved? What learning activities would we include in the course? Examine Figure 4.2 and assess the extent to which you agree with the different parts of it. Based on your own background, what changes would you make?

Figure 4.2 Example of backwards design in an ESP course for language teachers

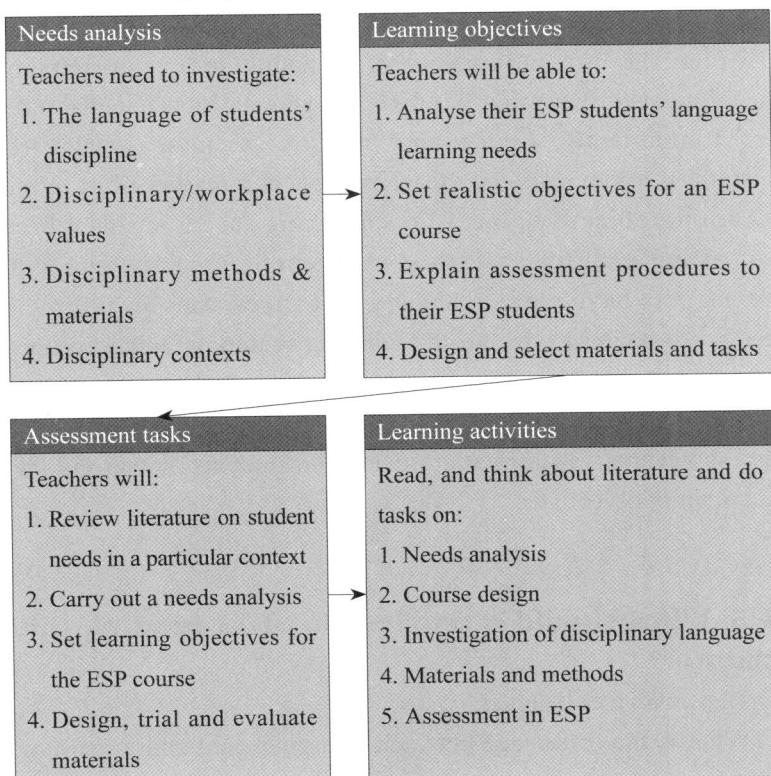

Needs analysis	Learning objectives
Teachers need to investigate:	Teachers will be able to:
1. The language of students' discipline	1. Analyse their ESP students' language learning needs
2. Disciplinary/workplace values	2. Set realistic objectives for an ESP course
3. Disciplinary methods & materials	3. Explain assessment procedures to their ESP students
4. Disciplinary contexts	4. Design and select materials and tasks

Assessment tasks	Learning activities
Teachers will:	Read, and think about literature and do tasks on:
1. Review literature on student needs in a particular context	1. Needs analysis
2. Carry out a needs analysis	2. Course design
3. Set learning objectives for the ESP course	3. Investigation of disciplinary language
4. Design, trial and evaluate materials	4. Materials and methods
	5. Assessment in ESP

4.4 Summary of the chapter

Curriculum development includes the planning, teaching and evaluation of the instruction for students. It involves the developers in moving back and forth between planning, teaching and evaluation until an appropriate curriculum is reached. Curriculum developers need to start by deciding the goals of the course, before deciding how these goals could be assessed. Only then could they plan the learning experiences and instruction.

To plan the curriculum, curriculum developers must take account of the learning context, the stakeholders' needs and, most importantly, the learners' needs. Curriculum developers also need to develop clear teacher goals and learner objectives. Learning objectives must be something that is measurable, for example during students' assessment. Once curriculum developers have clear goals and objectives, they would then be in a position to design the learning materials and activities for the course. The third step in the curriculum development process is evaluation of the curriculum, where the developers assess whether the curriculum meets the students' needs and the curriculum objectives.

4.5 What should a teacher do after reading this chapter?

Discuss with a colleague:

1. What is the difference between a teacher goal and a learning objective?

2. What is backwards design, and what is the reason that it is 'backwards'?

3. This chapter has said that the stages of curriculum design (planning – implementing – evaluating) are not linear. What is the reason for this?

Chapter 5

Approaches to curriculum design

┌─ **Pre-reading questions** ─────────────────────────────┐

Before you start reading this chapter, think about the following:

1) As an ESP teacher, which of the following would you think are important in the ESP curriculum? Place them in order from 'most important' to 'least important':

   • Grammar that is used in written and spoken language in your students' discipline or workplace

   • Vocabulary that is used in written and spoken language in your students' discipline or workplace

   • The genres of your students' discipline or workplace such as essays, emails, meetings etc.

   • Language functions such as making requests, invitations, refusals etc.

   • The content of your students' discipline or workplace

2) Which ones are most important in the ESP or language courses you are teaching or have taught previously?
└──┘

5.1 Introduction

Typically, ESP students are studying in tertiary contexts, although ESP in secondary contexts is also possible. ESP students are usually learning new content in their discipline at the same time as learning the language that is needed to talk or write about that content. This means that a structural curriculum, where the main focus is grammar and vocabulary, will not be appropriate. Although these are parts of an ESP curriculum, grammar and vocabulary need to be embedded in disciplinary content and taught as parts of a focus on key text types and academic skills. As far as possible, it is preferable to situate the learning of language in the content – genres (such as essays and reports), disciplinary academic skills (such as reading law cases or listening to lectures) or sociocultural functions (such as requesting information or leaving a message) that are likely to be used in activities and events in the students' disciplinary field or workplace. This chapter begins by considering a theme-based approach to curriculum design (Section 5.2). It then considers a curriculum that is based on important disciplinary or workplace genres (Section 5.3). Section 5.4 outlines an approach that builds the curriculum on academic skills. Section 5.5 summarises an approach depending on what learners need to communicate in the language. Section 5.6 introduces an approach embracing students' own input. Finally, this chapter will consider a curriculum in which the language instructor and the content instructor collaborate to design and team-teach a single course, making the

ESP course indistinguishable from the content course (Section 5.7).

Choice of which approach to use depends on the values of the teacher or curriculum designer, and their view of what constitutes language. In an ESP course, the teacher needs to investigate and understand the values and world view of the discipline. This process can be seen to a greater or lesser degree in each of the approaches that follows.

5.2 A theme-based approach

Theme-based or content-based courses are popular in English for Specific Purposes. Themes are content that is drawn from the students' discipline or workplace. Necessary language activities that are important in the theme are embedded into it. One benefit of a theme-based approach is that the course is contextualised in material that the learners are interested in, because it is useful to their disciplinary studies or their work. This promotes a sense of authenticity for the students and gives the course face validity with the learners, who view it as a course in their discipline rather than as a language course. A theme-based course involves use of disciplinary texts, and spoken events that are important in the discipline, and learners can acquire grammar and vocabulary incidentally through this contextualised use of language. For students, a theme-based course gives the sense that it is primarily content that is being acquired; for the teacher, however, the theme is the vehicle through which important language-related activities, genres that are important in the students' discipline or workplace, as well as necessary grammar and vocabulary can be taught. Below I describe a theme-based course that I designed and taught to first-year undergraduate science students (Parkinson, 2000).

This theme-based course for science students was designed to assist students in learning important genres they need for their science courses, as well as academic skills that are necessary for them to be successful in their studies and grammatical forms that are important in science. Important genres were descriptive/explanatory essays, laboratory reports etc. Academic skills that were embedded into the themes included reading scientific textbooks, writing science genres, listening to lectures, speaking to fellow students in small groups as well as giving short oral presentations.

One example of a theme in Parkinson's ESP course for science students concerns how wastewater is treated in order to sanitise it. Students gained background to the theme by reading a range of different texts. These included textbook extracts explaining the process of how wastewater is treated and news articles on sea and river pollution as a result of burst pipes or storm overflows. Academic skills based on this reading included note taking, paraphrasing, and integrating ideas from multiple sources. Students were also taken on a field trip to a water treatment plant, where they were given a guided tour. Skills associated with this field trip were listening to the expert who took them on the guided tour of the facility as well as asking the expert questions. Back in the classroom, students wrote their own account of wastewater treatment, as well as creating a flow diagram of the wastewater treatment process to promote their visual literacy. All these activities took around three weeks, about 12 hours of class time.

It should be noted that visual literacy is important in science; this can be seen in science research articles and science textbooks which use visual forms such as graphs, tables, schematic diagrams and photographs to explain scientific ideas in a different medium, allowing readers to visualise complex ideas. This makes visual literacy an important element of science literacy, which should ideally be included in a science ESP course.

It is observed that the academic skills of reading, writing, listening and speaking, as well as the language that is useful in talking and writing about science, are embedded in the theme/content. Thus, the theme-based approach to the curriculum can be seen to contain within it the academic skills approach which we will consider in Section 5.4.

Figure 5.1 Using the wastewater treatment theme to teach genres, visual literacy, reading, listening, speaking, writing and language

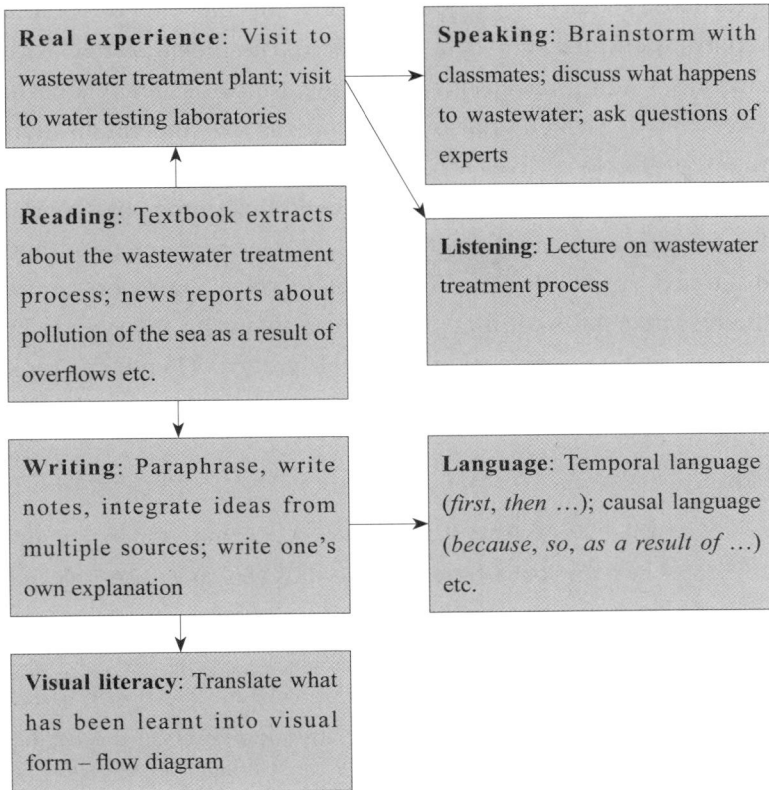

Real experience: Visit to wastewater treatment plant; visit to water testing laboratories

Speaking: Brainstorm with classmates; discuss what happens to wastewater; ask questions of experts

Reading: Textbook extracts about the wastewater treatment process; news reports about pollution of the sea as a result of overflows etc.

Listening: Lecture on wastewater treatment process

Writing: Paraphrase, write notes, integrate ideas from multiple sources; write one's own explanation

Language: Temporal language (*first, then* ...); causal language (*because, so, as a result of* ...) etc.

Visual literacy: Translate what has been learnt into visual form – flow diagram

A second example of theme-based teaching is drawn from a writing course for communications students. The students were first-years at a Chinese university who were taking a course that a colleague and I designed and taught. The theme concerns the social effects of the COVID-19 pandemic. It involved students in interviewing three classmates and then writing a report on the social effects of the pandemic on young people. This theme is relevant to communications students, who aim to become journalists. It allows them to get experience of writing interview questions, interviewing people, analysing the interviews and reporting on interview data in writing. The theme started with students reading about and discussing ethical issues related to interviewing, which is also important for the students in their future professional lives. The report genre was modelled for the students, who read and analysed several examples of reports. Useful language and important grammar were pointed out and discussed. Again, this theme embeds learning the report genre, the research skills of interviewing and analysing interviews, as well as reading and speaking in small groups. This theme took four weeks and involved 16 hours of class time.

Task 5.1

> With the ESP students that you teach or plan to teach in mind, think of a discipline-based theme that you could use. Think of the language demands of the theme. What reading, writing, listening and speaking can be embedded into the theme? What grammar and vocabulary are important for this theme? How does this focus on academic and language skills in the theme prepare students for learning other topics in their discipline?

5.3 A genre-based approach

A genre-based approach has been one of the most important approaches in English for Specific Purposes. The next chapter, Chapter 6, concerns teaching using a genre-based approach, so this section will provide only an introduction to genre-based teaching. With a genre-based approach, the teacher tries to identify the key genres that will be used to assess students in their discipline. For learners who are already employed, the teacher will identify the written and spoken genres that the learners need to use in their job.

Nesi's 2012 study of academic writing at British universities has shown how varied the genres students have to write are in different academic disciplines. This is depicted in Figure 5.2. Figure 5.2 shows that the predominant assignment type in the discipline of English is the essay. But the essay is hardly assigned at all in biological science and engineering, where the lab report is a far more frequent assignment type. Thus, an ESP teacher designing a curriculum based on genres for English majors would be justified in focusing on the essay genre. In business, by contrast, the ESP curriculum designer would need to include essay, case study and critique. In biological science, explanation, lab report and critique might be the focus of the curriculum and in engineering, lab report, case study, critique and design specification would likely to be the focus.

Figure 5.2 | Genres in four different academic disciplines (adapted from Nesi, 2012)

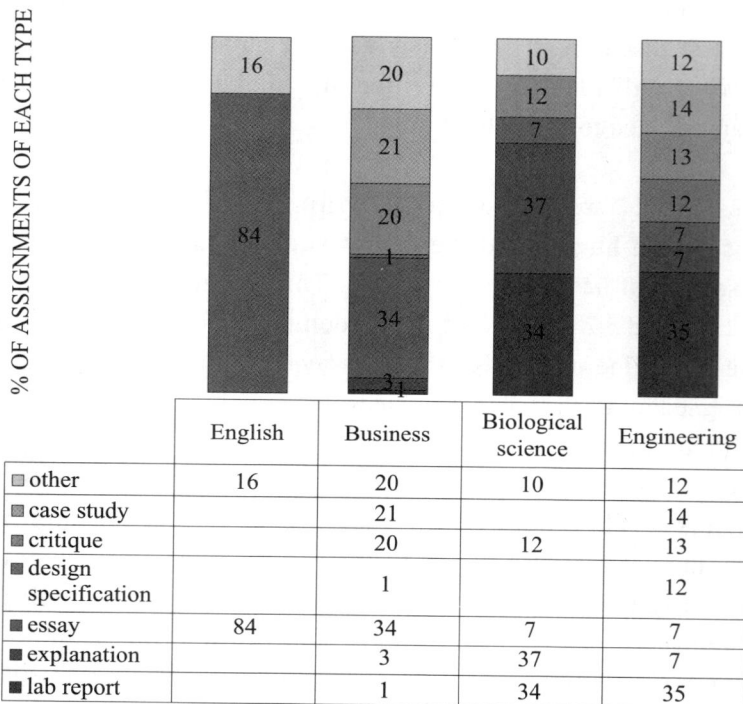

	English	Business	Biological science	Engineering
▣ other	16	20	10	12
▣ case study		21		14
▣ critique		20	12	13
▣ design specification		1		12
▣ essay	84	34	7	7
▣ explanation		3	37	7
▣ lab report		1	34	35

A genre-based approach would minimally familiarise students with the values of their discipline, and how the genre reflects the values of the discipline. For example, in science and engineering, the focus on the lab report is related to the empirically-based nature of the discipline, and a value system in which evidence in the form of measurements is important. In business and engineering, the case study is important because the ideas that are the subject of the case studies relate to events that have happened in the real world, from which students can learn. A second aspect of genre-based approach is related to teaching students the macro-organisation and linguistic features of the genres. An example of genre-based teaching can be found in Cheng (2006), who used a genre-based approach to teach graduate students to read and write research articles. As indicated above, the genre-based approach will be the subject of Chapter 6.

5.4 An academic skills approach

Some English for Specific Purposes courses prioritise the teaching of academic skills. This is particularly the case for courses that cater to groups of students doing a range of different disciplines. Often these courses are called English for Academic Purposes ones rather than ESP ones.

In an academic skills course, the skills of reading, writing, listening and speaking will be taught within the academic context. So, students might focus on strategies for reading textbooks or other reading materials that they need for their academic learning. This would include note taking, summarising and paraphrasing. The writing that will be the focus is the genres students need such as essays and reports. Lecture note taking would be the focus of listening skills, and short presentations on academic topics or taking part in discussions would be the focus of speaking skills.

Academic skills courses usually focus not only on the four skills of academic reading, writing, listening and speaking; they also focus on academic language functions, such as those based on Bloom's (1956) taxonomy in Table 4.2 in the previous chapter.

Teachers build into their curricula tasks that support students in dealing with the language demands of these academic language functions. They allow students to practise useful language and formulaic expressions related to the function (Christison & Murray 2021, p.176). For example, comparing and contrasting involve distinguishing the similarities and differences between two or more things. Useful language for them is comparatives such as *heavier, less heavy, more dangerous* and adjective phrases such as *similar to, different from* etc. Useful language frames can be provided and practised as well, such as *The function of _____ is similar to that of _____* or *Use of fertiliser A produced greater/less crop growth than use of fertiliser B* etc.

Task 5.2

How do you define academic language?

What academic language functions are particularly useful in a discipline of interest to you?

Select one of the academic language functions in Table 4.2 and identify useful language and expressions for expressing that language function.

5.5 A notional-functional approach

A notional-functional approach to teaching language and designing language curriculum is based on the consideration of what learners need to communicate in the language. What communicative functions will the learners need to engage in? These could be greeting others, offering help, making requests, apologising, making introductions or politely refusing to do something.

Curriculum designers using a notional-functional approach need to consider several aspects of the communicative context and the communicative functions that the learners will need in this context. These aspects are: the situation, including the participants and place; the topics that the learner will need to communicate about; the activity that the participants are engaged in, such as sales, teaching, answering the phone etc.; language functions such as greeting, inviting and requesting; ideas such as time (e.g. tense), quantity (e.g. countable/uncountable nouns) or likelihood (e.g. modal verbs); the grammar and vocabulary that the learner will have to use (e.g. 'Would you mind ...', 'Could you please ...' etc. for requests).

(Task 5.3)

Imagine that your students work or are training to work as salespeople in a clothing store. Consider the functions needed for this work.

1. Describe the situation (participants, relationship between them, and context).
2. List the topics the participants are likely to talk about.
3. What activity/activities do the participants engage in?
4. What language functions will the salesperson have to use?
5. What grammar will the salesperson need to use?
6. What useful vocabulary will be necessary?

An example of a notional-functional syllabus is the one designed in a study by Cowling (2007), which was discussed in Chapter 4. Cowling wanted to design a syllabus for new employees in a large Japanese industrial company. The company wanted an English language course that would help students adapt their current general English to business situations. The kinds of activities the new employees would need to engage in were introductions and greetings, hosting business visitors, business telephoning, giving presentations, and general small talk. Below is an example of a unit from Cowling's syllabus:

Figure 5.3 A unit in a notional-functional syllabus for a course for new employees in business (adapted from Cowling, 2007)

Language activity	Participants	Language functions	Classroom activities	Grammar and vocabulary
Calling a client	• Businessperson (company employee) • Receptionist at the company they are calling	• Introducing oneself • Asking to speak to someone • Leaving a message	• Listening tasks • Role plays • Discussions	Useful expressions and vocabulary, e.g. 'Could I speak to … please?'
Giving/taking orders	• Businessperson (company employee) • Businessperson at the client company	• Confirming details • Checking understanding • Requesting information	• Listening and writing tasks • Role plays • Discussions	Useful expressions and vocabulary, e.g. 'What is the estimated timeframe for delivery?'

5.6 A critical approach

Benesch (1999) suggests that in addition to analysing student needs, ESP teachers should also give attention to students' rights. Benesch examines a study in the context of a psychology course where about half the students, for whom English was a second language, were simultaneously enrolled in a paired EAP course, which Benesch herself taught. Benesch describes how in the psychology course there was little potential for dialogue between professor and students. The course covered a large amount of material, with no opportunity for in-depth discussion. There were also no tutorials where students could ask questions.

Benesch helped students deal with these difficulties by encouraging them to review their lecture notes. Because assessment involved multiple-choice tests, she encouraged students to write their own test questions and take each other's tests; each student also presented a topic from the textbook to the class. These activities supported students in meeting the demands of the course. However, in addition, Benesch supported students in challenging the requirements of the course, by their requesting additional help from the professor. Firstly, students thought of questions to ask the professor, despite there being little or no time in the psychology lectures allotted to student questions; secondly, Benesch asked the professor to visit the ESL class. This enabled a good discussion and allowed students to ask questions.

Benesch created further opportunities for students to develop a critical approach. She used research and writing assignments for the ESL students to do a more critical study of anorexia which had been briefly mentioned in a lecture. Moreover, students wrote and sent letters to the State governor explaining how a tuition increase and cuts in financial aid would affect them personally. Some also attended demonstrations.

What is your opinion of this critical approach to ESP? What potential do you see to use it in your own teaching?

5.7 Collaborating with disciplinary experts

As we saw in Chapter 2, in order to identify students' needs, the ESP teacher can collect information from various sources. One important source is disciplinary experts. Working with experts in the field is one of the most important ways for the ESP teacher to find out what students' language needs are. In addition to experts providing information about the language needs of their discipline, one approach to teaching ESP also involves collaborating with them to design and even teach the course. This collaboration can take a range of forms from no integration between the ESP teaching and the disciplinary teaching to full integration between them. At one end of the range, there is no collaboration between language teachers and disciplinary experts, and the language course and the content course are completely separate. At the other end of the range is a team-teaching situation, where a single course, focusing on both language and content, is designed by the language teacher and the content teacher, and both are present in the classroom. Language and content are taught simultaneously. An example of this model is found in Perry and Stewart (2005), described below. Between these two extremes of no collaboration and full collaboration is a situation in which the language teacher consults with the content teacher and then uses disciplinary content to teach language. An example of this model is found in Parkinson (2000), described in Section 5.2.

Dudley-Evans and St John (1998) suggest three levels of collaboration between language teachers and disciplinary experts. These are cooperation, collaboration and team-teaching. They describe these as follows:

- **Cooperation**: Language teacher gathers information about the subject course, and how English fits into it. They find out about the conceptual and discoursal framework of the discipline.
- **Collaboration**: Disciplinary teacher and language teacher work together outside of the classroom for language classes that prepare students to learn the disciplinary subject in English.
- **Team-teaching**: Disciplinary teacher and language teacher prepare classes and teach the class together.

An example of **cooperation** between language teachers and discipline experts is found in a study by Jackson (2005). Jackson conducted interviews with 45 business lecturers at five universities in Hong Kong, China. This allowed her to find out about the lecturers' experience of the students' English level. In her interviews she also investigated what the demands of the sub-disciplines of business courses were. For instance, she found that economics and accounting students were asked to write essays by their business lecturers, and they were tested with multiple-choice and short-answer questions. In contrast, law students and management and marketing students were assigned case studies to read and write.

An example of **collaboration** between ESP specialists and disciplinary experts is a study by Elder et al. (2012). Elder and her colleagues wanted to improve methods of assessment of a health-specific language test. The test involves role plays of health-related scenarios (e.g. taking a patient's medical history). Migrant doctors, nurses and physiotherapists need to take this test to achieve registration as a health professional.

The researchers' purpose was to identify the criteria used by health educators in judging the spoken clinical communication of student doctors, nurses and physiotherapists. Thirty-three educators from the three professions of medicine, nursing and physiotherapy took part in workshops. They viewed videos of trainees in their profession interacting with a patient. The educators took notes and then presented their comments orally. This enabled the researchers to identify the health educators' criteria for good communication of health professionals with patients.

Perry and Stewart (2005) stress that in order to maximise the benefits of **team-teaching**, there must be equality between the disciplinary teacher and the language teacher, and the two teachers must both be willing partners (not forced into partnership by their institution). The teachers need to be collaborative rather than competitive. One teacher in their study said:

> T1. '[A problem is] a sense of territoriality – I'm the language teacher and this is my area and you're not supposed to cross this boundary. And this is your area, content, and so you shouldn't expect us to cross each other. I think this kind of rigid boundary between content and language gets in the way of getting things done. ... because when you start thinking "well, this is my stuff and I want to see it work," ... as if it's a competition for who is the better teacher. This kind of ego involvement is in the way of actually serving the students.' (p.571)

Some teachers noted that through collaboration with the disciplinary specialist they came to see how difficult it was to separate the language from the content:

> T2. 'In this class ... the language is so integral with the content it's very difficult to draw a clear line.' (p.571)

They also noted that the two teachers must share a common pedagogical philosophy and an understanding of their roles and expectations in order for collaboration to be effective. The teachers interviewed in Perry and Stewart's study saw many benefits in team-teaching. For example, they claimed that the collaboration made them better teachers:

> T3. 'The main advantage I see in team-teaching is that with two teachers working together on a class, I have someone to bounce ideas off of, and vice-versa. I find it's made me very creative in that class.' (p.568)
>
> T4. '... ideally ... the language teachers are also teaching

> content at the same time, and the content teachers are teaching language. ... that makes both of them better teachers in the end.' (p.568)

Task 5.4

With the ESP students that you teach or plan to teach in mind, what disciplinary expert would you ideally work with?

What benefits and what difficulties do you predict you might experience by collaborating with a disciplinary expert?

5.8 Summary of the chapter

This chapter has discussed six different approaches to designing the ESP curriculum: a theme-based approach, a genre-based approach, an academic skills approach, a notional-functional approach, a critical approach and finally, a team-teaching approach. The most frequently used of these six are the first three: theme-based, genre-based and academic skills. In differing degrees, all approaches rely on relevant content or activities of the discipline, and language learning, such as the learning of genre, vocabulary and grammar, is embedded in these.

5.9 What should a teacher do after reading this chapter?

Think about which of these approaches to curriculum design would best suit your own experience, knowledge of the discipline, interests and students. Discuss your ideas with colleagues teaching ESP and try to map out a curriculum based on one of these approaches.

Chapter 6

The use of genre analysis in ESP

┌─ **Pre-reading questions** ─────────────────────

Before you start reading this chapter, think about the
following:

1) What is your definition of genre?

2) Can you think of any written genres?

3) Can you think of any spoken genres?

4) Are genres only found in academic contexts? Can
   you think of any genres found outside of academic
   contexts?

5) How do you go about teaching genre?

6.1 Introduction: what is genre?

What does the word 'genre' mean to you? Probably you can think of synonyms for genre such as 'type', 'kind' or 'style'. We are all familiar with genres in film, such as action films, horror films and romance. We are familiar with the plot lines and their variations, and we know which film genres we like and which we would never watch. Similarly with music, we are familiar with different genres such as rap, jazz, K-pop, country music and classical music. The same is true of literature. However, even in non-fiction there is a vast range of genres, from news to biography, to school textbooks. As language teachers, we are all familiar with written academic genres, such as essays, research reports, laboratory reports, literature surveys, case studies and proposals. Spoken academic genres include classroom teaching, lectures and student oral presentations.

In language classrooms, genre is often interpreted as being restricted to a focus on the structure or organisation of texts. However, this is a very limited view of genre. Genre researchers encourage us also to consider three important elements: audience, purpose and culture. Audience is very important, because depending on whom we are speaking to or writing for, we make changes to the way we communicate. These changes are subject to how well we know the person we are speaking to or writing for: compare the way you speak to a stranger and the way you speak to a friend. We also make changes based on the power differences between us and our addressee: consider how you speak or write to your boss and how you speak or write to a friend or student. Also, audience is important for another reason: it is helpful if we communicate in ways that are familiar to our hearers and readers. Take the example of applying for a job. We write the job application letter according to a particular style that we know is expected by potential employers. If we do not do so, our application is much less likely to be considered.

In fact, audience expectations are part of what creates genres. Tardy (2011, p.54) says that genres develop when people start responding to a specific need or purpose in ways that are similar to ways that other people have responded to that need or purpose. 'Responses begin to conform to prior uses until the shape of these responses **become[s] expected by the users**.'

Purpose is another important aspect of genre. If we think again of the job application letter, what is our purpose in writing the letter? On the one hand we could think of the purpose of such letters as being to communicate information about ourselves, such as our experience for the job, our qualifications etc. At a more global level though, our purpose in writing the letter is actually to get a job. In fact, Martin (1984, 1985), an influential author in the field of genre, stresses the important of purpose, saying that genres are 'goal-oriented purposeful activities' (Martin 1984, p.25). Martin also states that 'Genres are how things get done, when language is used to accomplish them' (Martin 1985, p.250). This means that we use a particular genre (e.g. job application letter) to achieve a particular purpose (e.g. getting a job).

Yet another important aspect of genre is culture. This can refer to different cultures in different countries. For example, we would expect job application letters to have some variation depending on the culture. But for our purposes as ESP teachers, we also need to consider the school culture, and how there may be variations in the cultures of different disciplines. If we compare the culture of science disciplines with the culture of humanities disciplines, we are likely to see differences, and these differences are likely to be reflected in the way we and our students write. In science, an important value is to be as objective as possible. In writing this is reflected in use of impersonal language. We would say 'The solution was poured into the test-tube' (not 'I poured the solution …'). Thus, in teaching students to write science genres we would explain why it is necessary to use the passive voice, and how that reflects the value of objectivity in science disciplines. In contrast, in the humanities an important value is being critical. This criticality can be reflected in the reporting verbs we use. For example, if we say 'Chen and Brown (2020) *claim* that …', the use of 'claim' suggests that we are not completely convinced of their claim. Inversely, if we say 'Smith and Brown *found* that …', the implication is that we accept what they say.

In using a genre-based approach to teach, it is advisable to start the teaching of the genre by helping students consider their audience (who they are writing for), their purpose in writing and the cultural values of the discipline in which they are writing. If we do this, students know who they are writing for, what the purpose of the writing is and how to ensure that their ways of expressing themselves align with the values of their discipline. By this means, we help students become part of their discipline.

Because genres address specific audiences and express the values of specific cultures, they are likely to use language that is quite specific in terms of vocabulary, grammar, language functions and discourse style. We saw this above in the discussion of how science writing uses impersonal language as a way of presenting itself as objective. An important genre researcher, Bhatia (2004, p.23), expressed this idea as follows: 'Genre essentially refers to language use in a conventionalised communicative setting in order to give expression to a specific set of communicative goals of a disciplinary or social institution, which give rise to stable structural forms by imposing constraints on the use of lexico-grammatical as well as discoursal resources.' This means that the purposes of a particular genre come to be expressed using a particular organisation, using a particular set of vocabulary and using particular grammatical conventions. We are also aware of how the formality of the language we use varies, depending on the genre we are writing. For example, a personal letter or an online blog will be less formal than a business letter or an academic essay.

Learning a genre is a lengthy process that requires learners to become part of the culture of a particular discipline or workplace. Learning a genre requires learners to learn when and how to use the genre, the likely content areas for inclusion in the genre, as well as the values and assumptions of the community that uses the genre (Berkenkotter & Huckin, 1993).

Task 6.1

Think about the medical community.

1. Who are the members of this community?

2. What are the values of this community? How would you go about investigating these values?

3. What genres are important for the medical community?

In response to Task 6.1, you may have suggested that the members of the medical community include not only doctors and nurses but other medical professionals as well, such as physiotherapists and dentists. What did you consider were the values of this community? Ideally, they include being caring and compassionate. They also include responsibility, competence and confidentiality.

6.2 The linguistic features of a genre

The linguistic features of a genre can be considered from two different perspectives. The first is structure or organisation, and the second is grammatical features and vocabulary.

6.2.1 Genre structure: move analysis

Teaching a genre often involves teaching learners the conventional organisation of the genre. For example, teachers will often provide learners with input on how to organise the introduction of an essay, with *context/background, importance of the topic, thesis statement* and *organisation of the rest of the essay* being common elements or **moves** that are included in teaching. These are shown in Table 6.1. Each of the moves in an essay introduction persuades the reader to read the essay, either by making it easier to read and understand or by stressing its importance and focus.

Table 6.1 Moves in an essay introduction

	Move in an essay introduction	Purpose of this move in an essay introduction	Example
Move 1	The context/ background of the topic	Makes the topic easier for readers to understand, because they know the general topic	In English for Specific Purposes teaching, the focus is on language that is needed in a particular discipline or workplace.
Move 2	Why the topic is important	Persuades readers that the essay is worth reading	This approach to language teaching has been growing in importance over the last 50 years.
Move 3	Thesis statement	Provides the focus of the essay	This approach is often more appropriate than general ELT, especially in tertiary contexts.
Move 4	How the rest of the essay is organised	Makes the essay easier for readers to understand, because they know what to expect	This essay will start by discussing the key features of ESP, before showing how these are reflected in three example ESP courses.

So what are moves? As we saw from the moves in Table 6.1, moves are pieces of a text that perform a particular purpose. Together the moves in a text fulfil the overall purpose of the text. We can see this in essay introductions. Each of the moves plays a part in introducing the essay and encouraging the reader to continue reading it.

In Table 6.2, we see an example of a student essay introduction[1]. Do you agree with the moves that have been suggested for each segment of the text? As we see, the *organisation of the rest of the essay* move has not been included in this introduction. Is it possible that this is an optional move? We would need to examine more examples of good student essays to find out if omitting this move is usual, or if this essay is an exception.

---

1 This example is taken from the Michigan Corpus of Upper-Level Student Papers (MICUSP), which contains assignments with a grade of A from the University of Michigan.

Table 6.2 Moves in a student essay introduction (from MICUSP)

Essay introduction	Move
The efficient allocation of resources has always been a <u>significant</u> topic in economics regardless of the context of the particular allocation. The illicit drug market is no exception. However, this market exhibits some <u>unique economic qualities</u> that <u>need to be called to attention</u> in order for proper consideration to be given for the allocation of resources to control this market. Drug use is often blamed for <u>a wide range of personal and social problems</u> including: loss of productivity, diminished health, moral degradation, excessive violence, the spread of disease, and many others.	Why the topic is important
Accordingly, our policy decisions have reflected our distaste for these consequences, and we have tried to outlaw drug-use altogether. However, as will be shown, the costs associated with these problems are tremendous,	The context or background of the topic
and <u>we must now call into question whether or not current forms of prohibition and resource allocation are an effective and efficient means of attacking these problems</u>.	Thesis statement
	How the rest of the essay is organised

A sample study that performs a move analysis is that by Henry and Roseberry (2001), who undertook an analysis of 40 job application letters. The study identified 11 moves, which are shown in Table 6.3. In Table 6.3, we can see that some moves occur more frequently than others and are described as obligatory moves, whereas other moves that occur less frequently are described as optional (Biber et al, 2007). Of these 11 moves identified by Henry and Roseberry, six were found in all 40 of the texts in their data set. These were thus obligatory moves. The other five moves in Henry and Roseberry's study occurred in fewer than 40 texts – they therefore saw these moves as optional.

Table 6.3 Moves in job application letters (based on Henry & Roseberry, 2001)

Move	Number of letters that contain the move
The writer identifies the addressee	40
The writer refers to the advertisement	40
The writer states an interest in applying for the position	40
The writer gives reasons for wanting the position	11
The writer indicates when he or she would be able to take up the position	2

(*to be continued*)

(continued)

Move	Number of letters that contain the move
The writer presents information demonstrating relevant qualifications and abilities	40
The writer indicates expectations regarding salary, working hours etc.	4
The writer names referees	2
The writer lists documents enclosed with the letter	34
Polite ending	40
The writer signs his or her name	40

6.2.2 The grammatical and lexical features of a genre

In their analysis of letters of application, Henry and Roseberry propose that in order to teach students to write this genre it would be useful to teach them the genre's linguistic features. They suggest that frequent phrases should be identified – e.g. 'I am very skilled with X', 'I am experienced in X', 'I am responsible for X'. They also suggest that use of frequent verbs, tenses, and other vocabulary and grammatical patterns in frequent moves should be identified.

To support acquisition of common grammar patterns, another study by Henry (2007) provided exercises for students to assist them in learning these patterns. For example, the study found that *to be considered* and *to apply* were common ways of *stating an interest in applying for the position*:

> I am writing **to be considered** for [name of job].
>
> I wish **to be considered** for [name of job].
>
> I would (very much) like **to be considered** for [name of job].
>
> I would like my application for [name of job] **to be considered**.
>
> I am writing **to apply** for [name of job].
>
> I wish **to apply** for [name of job].
>
> I would (very much) like **to apply** for [name of job].

6.3 How teachers can promote students' genre awareness

Genre awareness refers to the insight that a writer or speaker has about how to use the genre flexibly in response to their own purposes. In addition, genre awareness refers to the writer's or speaker's awareness that genres are not unchanging. They can and do change in response to changes in society or in the way that people achieve certain aims. One example is business communication, which rapidly changed from written letters to email communication. This change was in response to the development of the internet. Thus, genres can change in response to changing circumstances and changing needs. On the other hand, many genres are fairly stable, and they change only slowly. This is helpful because it makes genres predictable (Berkenkotter & Huckin, 1993).

Johns (2011, p.61) suggests that ESP teachers must develop in their students an awareness of genres as 'flexible and evolving'.

To foster sensitivity to the ideologies and values in disciplinary culture, genre-based teaching should encourage students to consider not only textual organisation, but the context in which a genre exists as well. Johns (1997) suggests that to develop student knowledge of the relationship between lexis, grammar, genre and purpose, and the relationship between reader and writer, the teacher can assign students the task of investigating these things by investigating their discipline. To do this, students can interview their professors to investigate topics like textual organisation and content, disciplinary argumentation and the professor's own disciplinary practices. Johns suggests encouraging students to observe and reflect on activities in their discipline, and to develop hypotheses about disciplinary culture.

Peacock (2002) also suggests ways for ESP teachers to foster genre awareness. His suggestion involves familiarising students with the moves of a genre. The first step will be for the teacher to discuss with students what moves are, why they are necessary and what they do. Teachers should use a discipline-specific move-structure model. They begin by providing students with a model text in which all moves are marked. They then ask students to describe the function of each marked move. Students then mark all the moves in a new text, before finally writing their own text in the genre.

An example of genre-based teaching can be found in Dong and Lu (2020). They used a three-phase approach to genre-based teaching including modelling of the genre, joint negotiation of the text and finally, independent construction of a text. Dong and Lu collected a corpus of 150 engineering article introductions.

These were analysed into rhetorical moves based on Swales (2004). Guided by the instructor, analysis was undertaken by the 30 master's students in the course as part of sensitising them to the genre. Students took part in genre-based activities. For example, students searched for a particular move, then identified linguistic expressions that were common in the move. A questionnaire to students at the end of the course showed that students felt that their knowledge of the rhetorical structure and linguistic features of engineering article introductions improved as a result of the course.

6.3.1 Teaching genre at school level

Australian genre theorists have given attention to teaching genre at school level. They focus on pedagogical genres, which are relatively short texts particularly common in primary school classrooms. Examples of these pedagogical genres are recount, narrative, procedure, information report, explanation, argument and discussion. Similar to move analysis, Australian genre theorists talk of the 'stages' or sections of a text.

Table 6.4 Pedagogical genres (adapted from Gibbons, 2015)

Pedagogical genre	Purpose of the genre	Organisation (stages)	Language features
Recount	To tell what happened; to document a sequence of events	Orientation Series of events Personal comment	Time connectors (e.g. *then*, *afterwards* ...) Past tense

(continued)

(continued)

Pedagogical genre	Purpose of the genre	Organisation (stages)	Language features
Narrative	To entertain and teach	Orientation Conflict/problem Attempts to resolve problem Resolution	Time connectors (e.g. *once upon a time*, *in the end*, *later* ...) Past tense
Procedure	To tell how to do something	Goal Steps in a sequence	Connectors (*first*, *second* etc.) Imperative mood
Information report	To present information about something	General statement Characteristics (e.g. size) Characteristics (e.g. types) Characteristics (e.g. development)	Use of subheadings for each characteristic Simple present tense
Explanation	To tell how and why things occur	Introduction Description in logical sequence	Generic participants Present tense action verbs Scientific lexicon

(to be continued)

(*continued*)

Pedagogical genre	Purpose of the genre	Organisation (stages)	Language features
Argument	To persuade; to argue a case	Statement of position Argument 1 Supporting evidence Argument 2 etc. Supporting evidence Conclusion	Connectors (*first, second* etc.; *however, therefore* etc.) Evaluative vocabulary
Discussion	To look at more than one side of an issue; to explore various perspectives	Statement of position Argument 1 (positive) Supporting evidence Argument 2 (negative) etc. Supporting evidence Conclusion	Connectors (*first, second* etc.; *however, therefore* etc.) Evaluative vocabulary

To teach writing using a genre-based approach entails teaching learners the stages, goals, and characteristic lexis and grammar of a particular genre. Some genres, such as the explanation genre, are very common in school, so it is very valuable for school children if they recognise the characteristic features of different genres. Table 6.4 shows the goals, organisation and language features of some important school genres.

To teach genre in primary school, teachers talk to learners about the purpose and audience of a text. They share the stages of the genre with their students, and students are given a vocabulary to talk about written genres. Teachers explore register (what?, who?, how?) as well as genre (why?).

Using the curriculum cycle, Gibbons (2015) discusses how genre is taught. This cycle will be repeated multiple times throughout a child's schooling. To build knowledge of the topic, the teacher and children will discuss the topic, read about it and generate questions they would like answers to. To model the text, the teacher will provide an example of this pedagogical genre and talk about the purpose and audience of the genre. The teacher will also draw attention to the organisation/stages of the text and look at typical language. In the third stage of joint negotiation, the teacher and children jointly write an example of the genre. The children will make suggestions for what to write while the teacher will write it down and guide the process by making suggestions and asking questions like 'What's the best way to say x?' or 'Can you think of a better word?' In the fourth stage, the children write an example of the genre on their own.

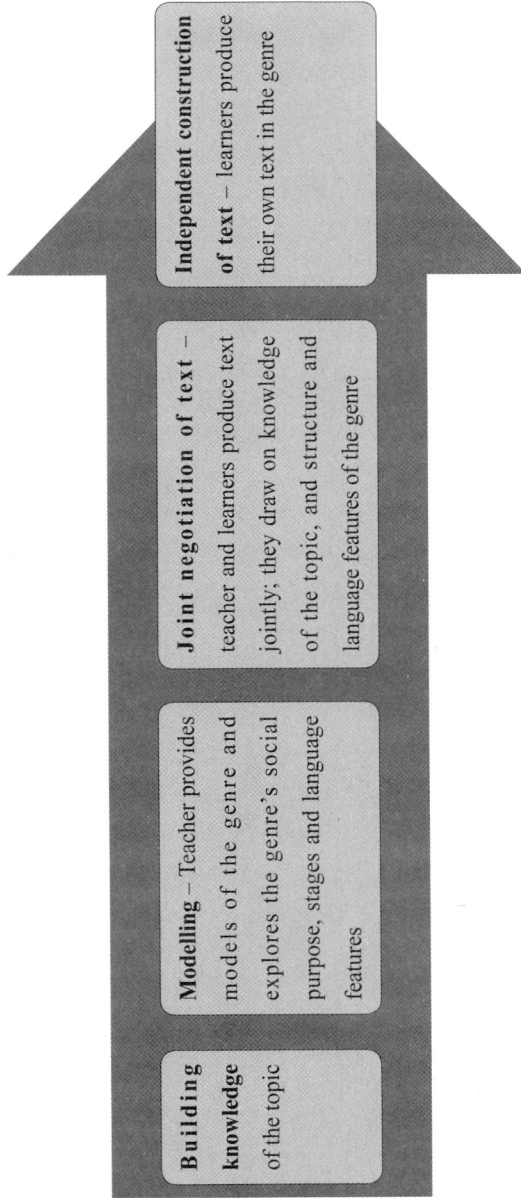

Figure 6.1   The curriculum cycle: scaffolding genre acquisition in the ESL classroom

Building knowledge of the topic

Modelling – Teacher provides models of the genre and explores the genre's social purpose, stages and language features

Joint negotiation of text – teacher and learners produce text jointly; they draw on knowledge of the topic, and structure and language features of the genre

Independent construction of text – learners produce their own text in the genre

6.4 Example of a written genre: email communication

Email communication is an extremely common genre taught in business communication courses. However, studies (e.g. Chan, 2014; Evans, 2012; Grosse, 2004; Warren, 2013) suggest that emails are often used together with telephone conversations. For example, Grosse (2004) found that emails and telephone conversations were used by the executives as the most common channels for communication. Several studies note that these written and spoken communication types may be used in conjunction with each other, with emails referring to telephone conversations and being used to confirm telephone conversations.

For example, Evans' (2012) study in the Hong Kong, China context offers practical suggestions about designing email tasks in Business English courses based on three data sources. These three sources were: 30 hours of interviews with English-using Chinese professionals, four case studies, and 50 email chains consisting of 406 separate messages. The study showed firstly that emails are often written before and/or after telephoning and other forms of spoken communication. Secondly, emails that are internal to the organisation are written with much higher frequency than external emails, and internal emails are less formal than external ones. Thirdly, emails are often short and straightforward; textbooks teach a three-part structure (opening, body, closing), but real-life email structure often gets to the point right away. Fourthly, workplace emails are written in chains in a back-and-forth manner, while textbooks tend to teach the first email of a chain only. The author suggests that email writing should be taught as integrated skills together with speaking, listening and reading. Evans also suggests a 'simulation-based approach' to teaching email writing; i.e. participants play differentiated roles in a particular business setting and are involved in business activities such as clarifying issues, arranging meetings, summarising documents in which email communication is used.

Another interesting study regarding emails focuses on their interpersonal aspects. Park, Jeon and Shim (2021) compared request emails written by South Korean and American professionals. Sixty emails were analysed and comparisons between the two email corpora were made regarding move frequency, move sequence and move length, together with lexical and syntactic complexity. The study showed that L2 professionals tended to make their requests more concisely using more direct language, whereas L1 professionals tended to use supportive moves such as promising compensation and offering compliments to their colleagues. Some important implications of this paper are firstly the importance of L2 professional writers giving attention to the use of small talk in writing business request emails. This is because small talk eases people into social interactions and can be essential for business communication. Secondly, Park et al. suggest that instruction on interpersonal communication should be part of L2 business email writing, including cultural considerations to improve how requests are experienced by the receiver.

6.5 Example of a spoken genre: nurse–patient communication

The nurse–patient interview is a medical genre that most of us who have visited the doctor or hospital are familiar with. Task 6.2 provides you with a short example of an interview and asks you to think about it from a genre perspective.

Task 6.2

A genre that is important for the medical community is the nurse–patient interview. Below is an example:

N: Hello my name is Maria, and I'm a nurse practitioner. What would you like me to call you?

P: Oh, I'm Melissa Smith, but Melissa is fine.

N: Can you tell me why you came to see me today?

P: My knee's been bothering me a lot.

N: Tell me more about the pain.

P: It's a throbbing pain. I get it throughout the day. If I walk too much.

N: When did it start?

P: A few weeks ago.

N: You say the pain is throbbing. Is there anything else about the pain?

P: No just throbbing.

N: What were you doing when it started?

P: I was walking upstairs at work.

N: On a scale of 1-10, 10 being the worst pain you've ever had, how bad is this pain?

P: Six or seven.

N: How often in a day does that happen?

P: Two or three times per day, whenever I walk upstairs or walk too far.

N: Can you point to where the pain is?

P: Here.

N: Is there anything that makes it feel better?

P: Nothing completely. I take a painkiller and it goes away for a while.

N: Are you taking any medication for anything else?

P: No, nothing.

N: Is there anything else you'd like to tell me today?

P: No, nothing else.

Discuss this example in terms of the following elements:

- Is it structured in stages or moves?
- What is its purpose?
- Who is involved in the interview?
- Do you notice any typical lexis, grammar or language functions that are used?

In Task 6.2, what were your thoughts about the stages or moves in the nurse–patient interview? The ones you thought of may have included:

- Greetings and introductions
- General questions to elicit main complaint
- Elicit history of present illness
- Elicit symptoms
- Questions regarding any other medical problems

The language functions in a nurse–patient interview that you might have thought of may have included *open-ended questions* and *avoidance of leading questions*.

Finally, you might have suggested that because medical personnel are speaking to patients who probably do not have any medical training, they use everyday language, not medical language or very formal language. Instead of saying 'Detrimental effects to health such as hypertension have been caused by tobacco use', which the patient might not understand, the medical professional might say: 'Smoking harms your body, and many people who smoke get high blood pressure.'

6.6 Summary of the chapter

This chapter started by considering the importance of audience, purpose and culture, and how these should be deliberated and discussed with students before teachers teach them the structure of a genre. Audience is important because it has an influence on the formality of the communication. A consideration of purpose is important because it allows writers and speakers to focus on what they are trying to achieve through the communication. Culture, whether national, ethnic or disciplinary culture, is important as it changes the way a genre is achieved.

The chapter also considered the idea of move analysis, which assists writers and speakers in organising their writing or speaking in the way expected by the audience. The chapter then considered how teachers can teach genre using move analysis. Finally, the chapter considered a written genre (email communication) and a spoken genre (nurse–patient interviews).

6.7 What should a teacher do after reading this chapter?

Try to list all the genres that your ESP students use in their content courses, whether it is a written genre or a spoken one. Pick one of those genres, and either do some reading to find out about the moves in the genre or examine several examples of the genre to work this out yourself.

Chapter 7

The contribution of register analysis to ESP

Pre-reading questions

Before you start reading this chapter, think about the following:

1) As an ESP teacher, how do you decide what grammar features to teach your students?

2) How do you decide what communication functions (such as requests, invitations, refusals etc.) to teach your students?

3) How do you decide what vocabulary to focus on?

7.1 Introduction

To guide ESP teachers in what language to teach, Basturkmen (2010) suggests that an important question that teachers need to ask is: What language (skills, genres and language features) do the learners need to know? To analyse learners' language needs, we know that a teacher or researcher can use a range of methods. In addition to finding already-published descriptions of learner language needs, teachers and researchers can use interviews, questionnaires, observation and text-based analysis. The previous chapter looked at one type of text-based analysis: genre analysis. This chapter considers a second kind of text-based analysis: register analysis. Both types of text-based analysis are important and are the basis of a good deal of materials design in ESP.

Register refers to the tone of writing or speech. Writers and speakers vary the way they express themselves. This variation depends on how well the writer knows their reader or how well the speaker knows their listener; it also depends on how formal the writing or speech is, on what the purpose of the writing or speech is and on the kind of occasion at which the writing or speech is being used. Writers and speakers vary the register of what they say through their choice of vocabulary and phrases, as well as their grammar.

How can the teacher or researcher investigate the register of a particular kind of text? One approach is to draw on corpus data. Sinclair (2004) defines a corpus as 'a collection of [...] texts in electronic form, selected [...] to represent [...] a language or language variety'. An important use of corpora has been for dictionaries and grammars. An example is Biber et al.'s *Longman Grammar of Spoken and Written English* (1999), which describes the grammar of English by drawing on four registers: conversation, academic writing, written and spoken news, and fiction.

For teachers of university students who want examples of how good students write a particular genre, there are existing corpora of the writing of students who achieved good grades. These include the Michigan Corpus of Upper-Level Student Papers (MICUSP), which is a 2.6-million-word corpus of texts that were written by students at the University of Michigan and awarded A grades. Another written corpus is the British Academic Written English Corpus (BAWE) collected at three British universities which is about 6.5-million words. The MICUSP can be used for both teaching and research, but the BAWE can be used for research only. These corpora are extremely useful for ESP teachers who want to find out about student writing in a particular discipline or genre. The MICUSP and BAWE have been classified into assignment/genre types (e.g. essay, laboratory report, critique, proposal etc.). They are also classified according to the discipline in which they were written. Equivalent spoken corpora are the Michigan Corpus of Academic Spoken English (MICASE) which contains about 1.8 million words, and the British Academic Spoken English Corpus (BASE) of approximately 1.6 million words.

ESP teachers can also use general corpora such as the British National Corpus (BNC) which is 100 million words and was collected 1980s–1993, or the Contemporary Corpus of American English (COCA) which is 440 million words from 190,000 texts (collected 1990–2012) and contains about 88 million words each of spoken language, fiction, magazine, newspaper and academic language. However, ESP teachers must take care when using these large general corpora to select language that is related to the discipline or profession you and your students are interested in.

Teachers may have access to small, specialised corpora consisting, for example, of the genre that they or their students are interested in. They may collect examples of a particular student genre. With the permission of the student writers, writing that achieved high grades might be used as examples for students. It is not advisable to write the examples yourself, because, as we know, purpose and audience matter in genre studies. As a teacher, you have a different purpose and audience from a student, and thus without you being aware of it, the text you write as an example may not be representative of the genre.

(Task 7.1)

Log in to the MICUSP (https://elicorpora.info/main) and select the discipline and genre you are interested in (e.g. argumentative essays in English; reports in biology; proposals in nursing etc.).

7.2 Contribution of register analysis to teaching disciplinary texts at school

Several studies have focused on the value of sensitising school children to the register features of the texts they need to read or write. To provide examples of this, this section will look at a study of primary age children by Wollman-Bonilla (2000), and then at a study of middle school children by Schleppegrell and Achugar (2003). From these two studies we can see that register analysis is useful in teaching school children as well as students at tertiary level.

Wollman-Bonilla (2000) looked at how teachers of children in the first grade of primary school scaffolded children's acquisition of the scientific register. The author studied classrooms where the teachers guided the children to write a genre called the Family Message Journal. This was a short account of science investigations and experiments that the students or teacher had done in the classroom. Children wrote the journal to take home to their families. Because the family members had not been present in the classroom to see what had happened, there was a need for the child to explain and be explicit about it (e.g. using nouns instead of pronouns to name the objects involved and describe them). Thus, the Family Message Journal functioned to shift the children from the register of speaking face to face to a register that is more appropriate in writing, where there is a need to name things and be explicit.

Figure 7.1 shows an example of an explanation text written by a child in Wollman-Bonilla's study. We can see that the child has organised her text according to the stages of the explanation genre (Introduction, Description in logical sequence), which we saw in Table 6.4 in the previous chapter. The child has also used the language features of science, including generic rather than specific participants and the simple present tense (such as *help* and *give*), which is used to express general truths. She has also used formal scientific vocabulary. [It should be noted that the child was in the first grade of school, so the spelling errors can be expected, particularly for the scientific vocabulary which might be new to the child.]

Figure 7.1   Use of science register by a child in the first grade of school (Wollman-Bonilla, 2000)

Genre: stages of the explanation	Explanation	Register: features of the science register
Introduction	Dear Family Trees help us breath.	Generic participants (*trees, air*)
Description in logical sequence	And if you put a bag over your face you can suficate and die. And did you know we help the trees breath we breath out carbon dunockside and give it to the trees and the trees give us air to Love Sara	Present tense action verbs (*help, breath, put, suficate, die, give*) Scientific lexicon (*suficate, carbon dunockside*)

Wollman-Bonilla reports that the teachers scaffolded the children's learning by discussing the content that the children could include in their Family Message Journals. The teachers also modelled the kind of language that the children could use, and they encouraged use of scientific words. They encouraged the children to talk about what they would write, providing an oral rehearsal for the writing.

A second interesting study by Schleppegrell and Achugar (2003) concerns how teachers scaffolded learning of the register of history by middle school children. They note that for school children a difficulty of learning to read history texts is that in history texts people are usually represented as groups (e.g. *scientists, the allies, the peasants, government officials, Americans* etc.) rather than as individuals. This makes it harder for the students to work out who the text is about. Events are often expressed by means of nouns (e.g. *revolution, economy, proclamation* etc.) rather than by verbs, which are more expected when we are talking about actions. The teachers in Schleppegrell and Achugar's study therefore focused on improving their students' ability to read history texts by identifying what happened, who the people involved were and what the power relations were between these people.

7.3 Contribution of register analysis to teaching vocabulary in a university course

An important value of register analysis is in identifying the technical vocabulary of a discipline. For example, Coxhead and Demecheleer (2018) used a corpus of written coursebooks in the vocational discipline of plumbing, as well as recordings of plumbing teaching. In addition, this study relied on specialist informants, the plumbing teachers, to judge if words were technical ones or everyday ones. They identified 97 technical words, including *pipes*, *flow*, *maintenance* and *sealant*. This approach of asking experts such as subject teachers if a word is technical is a useful one. However, ESP teachers should not feel a responsibility to teach their students technical vocabulary, because these words often represent conceptual knowledge that they do not possess. It is better for ESP teachers to support their students in acquiring techniques for finding out the technical meanings or to work with content teachers to develop glossaries.

Another study of technical vocabulary is that of Bancroft-Billings (2020), who used corpus methods to identify spoken technical legal vocabulary. The aim of the study was to find useful spoken technical legal words to introduce to ESL students who were undertaking law studies in the US, therefore improving their ability to understand classroom lectures and discussions. Focusing on the vocabulary of a first-year Contracts course, data collected consisted of transcripts from recordings of all class meetings, written texts for the course, as well as class observations. Spoken technical legal vocabulary was identified, and 290 words were found to fall into this category. Examples are *appeal*, *claimant*, *debtor*, *endorsement*, *forfeiture*, *infringement*, *liability* and *malpractice*. Bancroft-Billings analysed language-related episodes, where focus of discussion in the law class was on language. These were often about definitions. The example below shows how law professors focused on and talked about vocabulary in these law classes, and how students learnt the vocabulary in context. The teacher not only defined the term, but also provided the analogy with adhesive tape to stress the meaning of this term:

> Professor K: So, we actually have a name for this kind of agreement in contract law. The agreement that is prepared by one party in advance of the transaction and is offered to you on a take it or leave it basis, we call it a **contract of adhesion**. Like it sticks to you like Scotch Tape: **contract of adhesion**.

Bancroft-Billings found that most language-related episodes concerned definitions. Others concerned language control (use of language in the right way), clarification, interpretation (e.g. of ambiguous language), mechanics (e.g. syntax or pronunciation) and pragmatics (e.g. cultural appropriateness). In this study, Bancroft-Billings was focusing on attention paid to language by the content teacher. A similar focus is found in Basturkmen and Shackleford (2015) who drew their findings from an accounting classroom, and in McLaughlin and Parkinson (2018) who studied carpentry teaching.

7.4 Contribution of register analysis to course development for workplace training

A study by Cutting (2012) focuses on the development of materials for English courses for airport ground staff. Ground staff need to be able to communicate in English with passengers or pilots. The ground staff worked at an airport in France. They needed to be able to communicate in English with the passengers they came into contact with. The researchers observed security guards, bus drivers, catering staff and ground handlers doing their jobs; they took notes of dialogues, frequently-used expressions and typical scenarios. However, for security reasons the researchers could not record these interactions.

Semi-authentic dialogues were built by linguists and language teachers who had extensive experience of ground staff discourse. These were checked by ground-staff managers and trainers. Course materials were based on an analysis of the semi-authentic dialogues and they centred on politeness features and functions such as requests and apologies. An example is included in Figure 7.2, showing an interaction between a security guard (SG) and a passenger (P). Focusing on the phrases that have been italicised or underlined, we can see the multiple uses of imperatives (*take off*, *put*, *step forward*), as well as ways that directives have been made more polite (*please, can, just, I'm sorry, I'm afraid*). It is also clear how the security guard gradually escalates their attempts to get the passenger to cooperate. At first the security guard uses polite expressions to try to persuade the passenger to cooperate. When the passenger refuses to comply, the security guard tries to persuade them by mentioning *international regulations* and the *random* nature of the check. Only when they are unable to get cooperation from the passenger do they threaten to call the *police officer*.

Figure 7.2 Typical scenario between airport security guard (SG) and passenger (P) (adapted from Cutting, 2012)

SG: Please *take off* your coat and *put* it in the basket.

P: OK. [P puts coat in basket, walks forward and stops before the archway]

...

[P goes through the archway. The alarm sounds]

SG: <u>Can</u> you go through again and *take off* your belt?

...

SG: I'll <u>just</u> have to give you a search. *Step forward* a bit.

P: Why?

SG: <u>This is just a random check</u>.

P: Look, I've been waiting here for 30 minutes. Can we just skip this? [P waves her arms around. SG remains still]

SG: <u>I'm sorry</u>. <u>This is part of international regulations</u>. <u>It'll take a minute</u>.

P: I'm sorry. I'm not going to stand here and miss my flight.

SG: OK. I'll have to call a police officer, <u>I'm afraid</u>. [SG reaches for his walkie-talkie]

Limitations of Cutting's method were that Cutting and her colleagues could not record interactions because of security concerns. As a result, Cutting's dialogues were invented. They were based on the linguists and language teachers' experience. They could therefore be atypical in some way. Also, the 'corpus' of dialogues was extremely small: less than 1000 words for the airport security guards, for example.

7.5 Contribution of register analysis to teaching grammar and register of professional discourse

This section uses the example of nursing discourse to illustrate the contribution of register analysis to the teaching of professional discourse. In western countries such as the US and New Zealand, very high proficiency levels are required for nurses whose first language is not English to practise the nursing profession. In spite of this, patients sometimes complain about communication difficulties. The studies below suggest that it is not that the nurses lack English proficiency, but that according to the patients, the nurses show little empathy and rapport with them. It is possible that the nurses have other ways of showing empathy based on their L1, and they may be unaware of ways of how the local nurses show empathy in English in the local context.

One study that is very useful for ESP teachers of nursing students who speak English as a second or foreign language and who need to interact with native speakers is by Staples (2015). Staples collected a corpus of recorded nurse–patient interactions. Her study involved nurse–patient interactions between patients and 52 internationally educated nurses (most of them from the Philippines) and 50 US ones. The patients were actors trained to play the part of a female patient in her 50s with a history of diabetes and high blood pressure. The interactions between nurses and patients were recorded and transcribed, and these formed the corpus. The internationally educated nurses contributed about 37,000 words, and the patients speaking to internationally educated nurses contributed about 14,000 words. In the study, the researcher identified features that the nurses used to express involvement, such as first and second person pronouns, hedges (e.g. *kind of, only*) and conditionals (e.g. '*If you are in pain, see Dr Carl*'). She also identified narrative features such as use of past tense, as well as stance features such as modal verbs (e.g. *will, should, can*), adverbs (e.g. *surprisingly, obviously*) and *that*-complement clauses (e.g. *'I just hope that I've plugged it in properly'*).

The internationally educated nurses were highly proficient in English and there was no evidence of communication difficulties. Differences between them and the US nurses were largely related to ways of showing empathy and rapport. The US nurses created a more patient-centred environment and used more reassuring language. Staples reports that the internationally educated nurses used fewer softening devices, and fewer phrases to express empathy. Some of her findings are shown in Figure 7.3. Staples suggests that discussion of the language used to create patient-centred interactions as shown in Figure 7.3 might be useful for the internationally trained nurses.

Figure 7.3 Some differences between the language used by internationally educated nurses and US ones

	Internationally educated nurses	US nurses
Softening devices	Fewer prediction modals 'Let me check your feet'	More prediction modals 'I'm *going to* feel your pulse'
	Less hedging 'It was the Nexium'	More hedging '*Maybe* it was the Prilosec'

(*to be continued*)

(continued)

	Internationally educated nurses	US nurses
Expressing empathy	A focus on physical issues rather than on psychosocial issues	More focus on psychosocial issues such as bereavement
Building rapport	Stance *that*-clauses to issue directives 'Make sure you don't eat food which is fat'	More stance *that*-clauses to reassure patients 'I'll make sure the social worker comes to see you'
		More stance verbs + *to*-clauses to suggest course of action 'If you **want** to have one of our priests'
	Stance adverbs to focus on plan of care 'Maybe we can repeat an EKG'	More stance adverbs to express empathy 'I would say maybe talk to a counsellor' 'I kind of know what you're going through'

Using the same corpus of nurse–patient interactions as that described above, Staples (2019) reports on the development of a pronunciation course for internationally educated nurses. Three pronunciation features were analysed: pitch range, tone choice and prominence, and the study found big differences between the two groups of nurses regarding these three pronunciation features. For example, although very similar phrasing was used by both groups for greetings and expressions of empathy, a difference was that the US nurses used a narrower pitch range for greetings, but a much wider pitch range for empathetic responses than the internationally educated ones did. Wider pitch range was associated with the nurse sounding more empathetic. Moreover, the internationally educated nurses were more likely to use a level tone when expressing empathy, while the US ones were more likely to use a falling tone.

The internationally educated nurses also stressed more words (45%) than the US ones did (25%). Staples comments that too many stressed words can be tiring to listeners, and they can also make the nurse sound irritated. Examples of this difference, with stressed words underlined, are shown below:

> US nurse: <u>Sometimes</u> those kind of medications like that they <u>decrease</u> the <u>acid</u>. And they don't work <u>right</u> away. It takes a few doses to <u>actually</u> you know they work a <u>little</u> bit and but it takes a few doses to <u>actually</u> get them working <u>totally</u>. (p.20)
> Internationally educated nurse: <u>Here</u> in <u>our</u> in <u>our</u> place <u>here</u> on <u>this floor</u> we <u>check</u> the <u>sugar four times</u>. (p.20)

A pronunciation course was then designed, which aimed to better internationally educated nurses' interaction with patients by improving their understanding of the sound system of American English. It aimed also to improve understanding of aspects such as stress and intonation. The course was then evaluated, and it was found that the materials used in the course resulted in improvements in the use of specific pronunciation features for purposes related to politeness, rapport and empathy. The nurses' opinions on the materials were positive.

Ferguson (2001) also investigated medical discourse focusing specifically on *if*-conditionals which were found to be quite frequent during doctor–patient consultations, with 77 uses in 34 consultations. About half of the uses in doctor–patient interactions related to hypothetical meanings (e.g. '*If you were to ask me is it safe to go out to work, yes sure*') and the other half were pragmatic: ways of using polite directives when speaking to patients (e.g. '*If you go outside, Sister will fix things up*'). Hypothetical meanings were also found in written medical texts, but pragmatic meanings were not. This suggests the usefulness of teaching medical students the pragmatic use of conditionals in spoken interaction with patients.

7.6 Teaching register features

A number of studies describe using corpora for ESP teaching of register features of texts. One interesting study by Noguera-Díaz and Pérez-Paredes (2019) concerns the teaching of Spanish seamen who work in military submarines. The authors note that little is known about the language registers that the military are exposed to. They compiled a corpus of naval submarine English from magazines and journals in the Navy. They then focused on the register features of noun phrases (e.g. *submarine rescue ship*; *system design issues*), and considered the ten most frequent nouns: *submarine, system, Navy, ship, boat, force, capability, class, missile, torpedo*. They found that a high proportion of nouns in their corpus was preceded by premodifiers, and that nouns were very frequently used as such (e.g. *antisubmarine warfare programmes*). This makes processing these noun phrases complex. The authors suggest the value of drawing on their corpus to provide students with exposure to patterns of noun phrases and experience in how to use them.

A study by Cheng (2007) concerns the teaching of the language features of research articles. Cheng's students were graduate students in an academic writing course. Most of them were doctoral students studying a range of disciplines from engineering to finance to agriculture. As doctoral students, most of the texts they read were research articles, and they were also expected to write those, so it was important for them to be sensitive to the organisation and register of research articles. Students collected five or more research articles in their field. Teaching involved discussions of research article sections. Cheng asked students to consider questions like 'What is the author trying to do?' (p.291) in a particular section of a text. Students were also asked 'What words and phrases were used to achieve this purpose?' Cheng assigned out of class genre awareness tasks in which students independently analysed rhetorical organisation and lexico-grammar of selected parts of texts and reflected on how particular purposes were achieved in their own discipline.

For Cheng genre awareness included the ability to recognise particular generic features and then use them in new rhetorical contexts in order to create particular reader responses. Also important was student awareness of the roles of writer, reader, purpose and use in genre production.

Charles (2014) also reports on ESL students' use of self-built corpora over a 12-month period. Students were enrolled in a course where they learnt to build their own corpus of disciplinary articles for academic writing purposes. The author used a questionnaire survey to find out students' experience of using their corpus. Most of the students used their corpus (70%). Students used their corpus for the main purpose of checking grammar and vocabulary during composing and revising their writing.

7.7 Summary of the chapter

This chapter has introduced how teachers can focus on teaching the typical language features (register) of a genre. Register is different if we compare different types of writing or speaking (e.g. academic writing compared with fiction, or lectures compared with casual conversation). Importantly for ESP teachers, register can vary depending on discipline. Teachers can use corpora of student writing that achieved high grades to identify the features of writing in the students' discipline, in order to help teaching register to their students.

7.8 What should a teacher do after reading this chapter?

It is clear that teachers usually do not have the time or expertise to undertake the kinds of register studies that have been described in this chapter. What is very useful, though, is for teachers to check whether any studies have been done concerning the discipline or genre that they are teaching. Teachers can try to access these studies to guide them in what register features of the language they plan to teach. If this is not possible, teachers can do simple investigations for themselves, such as the one below in Task 7.2.

Task 7.2

Log in to the MICUSP (https://elicorpora.info/main) and select a discipline that is of interest to you.

What genre is most common in this discipline in the MICUSP?

Select five texts from this discipline and genre.

Look at the first paragraph of each one.

Do you find any similar language features (e.g. do these first paragraphs mention the aim/purpose/goal/function of the text)?

Chapter 8

Materials development in ESP

┌─ **Pre-reading questions** ─────────────────────┐

Before you start reading this chapter, think about the
following:

    Given what you know about the field of ESP, what key
    features do you expect will be associated with ESP
    teaching materials?

└──┘

8.1 Introduction

There are a number of textbooks and articles on how to develop general language teaching materials, but can these help us in developing materials for ESP? For example, Tomlinson (2010) outlines principles for language teaching and language acquisition (see Table 8.1). But how does ESP align with Tomlinson's principles for general language teaching? So far, this book has suggested some key principles as being important in ESP, and Table 8.1 maps these on to Tomlinson's language teaching principles and language acquisition principles. The first of the principles that are important in ESP is the principle discussed in Chapter 1, that language teaching should be as specific as possible to the target discipline or workplace. As we can see, Tomlinson also suggests that relevance to the local situation is important, so this has some alignment with the focus on specificity and the students' discipline in ESP.

A second key principle of ESP is that a focus on learner needs is essential, as discussed in Chapter 2. In ESP, enabling learners to function in the target language in the target discipline or workplace is paramount, because studying their discipline or employment in the workplace is the reason that learners are learning the language. This corresponds to Tomlinson's second language teaching principle, that content and methodology should meet the learners' needs and wants. It also aligns with his language acquisition principles relating to cognitive and affective engagement and his requirement that language learning be relevant and interesting. If teaching materials are specific to the learners' discipline or workplace, they are more likely to be engaged in what they are taught.

A third ESP principle is the importance of basing language teaching materials in the content of the discipline or workplace. As mentioned in Chapter 1, drawing on learners' disciplinary content increases their interest in and enjoyment of their language learning. This focus on content areas is another principle for language teaching in general that is mentioned by Tomlinson; it is also relevant to another of Tomlinson's language acquisition principles: that learners should be exposed to meaningful and comprehensible input.

A fourth ESP principle involves a focus on the language features of disciplinary or workplace texts, whether at the level of organisation or of register. These were the focus of Chapters 6 and 7, and align with Tomlinson's language acquisition principles of encouraging noticing of language features in input and also giving learners opportunities to achieve communicative purposes.

Thus, we can see that key principles of ESP are well aligned with the principles of general language teaching that Tomlinson lists. In this chapter we focus on how these can be put into practice in ESP materials.

Table 8.1 Principles for language teaching and language acquisition (from Tomlinson, 2010) compared with key principles of ESP stressed in this book

Language teaching principles	Language acquisition principles	Key principles of English for Specific Purposes in this book
• Make the materials relevant to the local situation		• Language teaching should be as specific as possible to the target discipline or workplace (Chapter 1) • The focus of teaching should be disciplinary or workplace speech events; disciplinary or workplace texts; disciplinary or workplace activities (Chapter 5) • Help learners acquire disciplinary or workplace values (Chapter 3)
• Content and methodology should meet the learners' needs and wants	• Ensure that learners are engaged cognitively and affectively • Aim for learners to achieve positive affect – so as to make language learning enjoyable, relevant and interesting	• Focus on learner needs: enabling learner to function in the target language in the target discipline/workplace is very important (Chapter 2)

(to be continued)

(continued)

Language teaching principles	Language acquisition principles	Key principles of English for Specific Purposes in this book
• Focus on content areas and transferable skills	• Expose learners to a rich, meaningful and comprehensible input of language in use	• Base language teaching materials in the content of the discipline/workplace (Chapter 1)
	• Encourage noticing of salient features of input • Give learners repeated opportunities to use language to achieve communicative purposes	• Teaching should give attention to organisation of disciplinary or workplace texts (Chapter 6: genre analysis) • Teaching should give attention to the language of disciplinary or workplace texts (Chapter 7: register analysis)

8.2 The process of materials development

In a chapter on ESP materials design, Bocanegra-Valle (2010) lists several important considerations for the ESP materials developer.

- What is the target topic or content of the materials?
- Is this topic relevant for the students and for the discipline?
- What do the students know about the topic?
- What does the ESP teacher know about the content?
- Do the materials reflect the language conventions of the discipline?
- What are the learning goals?
- What is the target language form (lexical or grammatical feature), function (e.g. questions, apologies etc.) or skill (e.g. writing, speaking etc.)?

Because developing new materials is time-consuming, Bocanegra-Valle suggests that the teacher's first step be to investigate what materials are already available, suitable and accessible. Her proposed process for developing new materials and adapting existing materials is shown in Figure 8.1.

Figure 8.1 The process of ESP materials development (adapted from Bocanegra-Valle 2010, p.145)

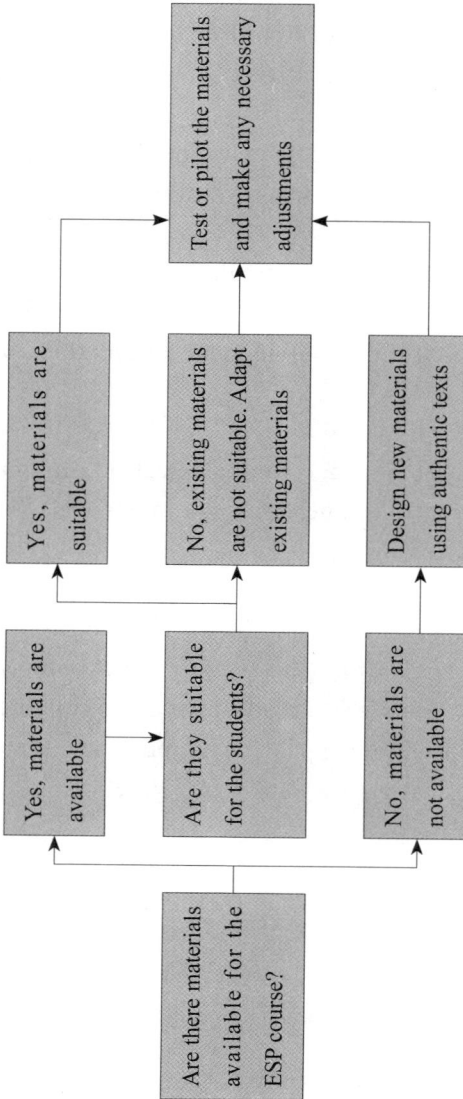

Techniques for adapting existing materials include removing parts of the materials, simplifying a text or an activity to make it more suitable for learners, adding to the existing materials, or replacing parts of the existing materials (Bocanegra-Valle, 2010).

8.2.1 Why would available materials be unsuitable?

Many studies have been done to investigate mismatches between textbooks and learner needs. Below we consider some studies that evaluated textbook materials using existing research and their own research to do so. Existing research is important. Chan (2009) notes that when we evaluate existing materials, it is important to first review research that is relevant to the context and to the register, skills or genre that we want to teach. This will enable us to judge whether the materials are relevant to our students.

A study by Cheng, Lam and Kong (2019) considered linguistic devices of interpersonal communication in workplace English as reflected in ESP textbooks designed for senior secondary students in Hong Kong, China. They note that earlier research (Koester, 2010) analysed a corpus of American and British office talk and outlined four areas of workplace communication that were important: expressing stance, hedging and politeness, showing and building shared knowledge, and showing empathy and solidarity. Cheng et al.'s study aimed to determine to what extent textbooks reflect real-life workplace communication. Four commercial textbooks were analysed by the use of a theme-based approach. They found that showing empathy and solidarity, as well as showing and building shared knowledge, is insufficiently attended to in textbooks. In addition, the study also found a mismatch between the genres included in textbooks and those that are important in the workplace. Textbooks were found to focus on phone calls, letters of complaint, and replies to letters of complaint. However, they did not pay enough attention to making and handling telephone complaints, CVs, emails, sales letters and job application letters which are used frequently in the workplace. This study recommends that ESP teachers should supplement textbook materials when teaching interpersonal language.

Another study by Lam, Cheng and Kong (2014) evaluated how a textbook module on interpersonal communication prepares students for workplace communication. It compared textbooks with corpus data and found discrepancies between the two data sources regarding the genres included in the textbooks and those matching learner needs. Similarly, mismatches were found regarding linguistic features included in the textbooks and those required by learners. They concluded that materials developers should give more attention to the specific workplace context that learners will move to after graduating. They suggest that, if possible, corpora should be used to provide authentic workplace discourse as the basis of materials.

Bocanegra-Valle (2010) suggests several considerations in designing new ESP materials or adapting existing ones. Firstly, the ESP materials designer needs to balance language and communicative content. The topic should be of academic, professional or workplace interest. For tertiary-level or secondary-level students, the topic of the materials should be linked to students' content courses. Materials should cover both language and skills. The language skills included depend on learner needs. Although we can consider the four skills of reading, writing, listening and speaking in this, the materials designer would of course prioritise the skills that learners need. Some learners may mainly have needs for reading in English (e.g. some students), while others' main needs may be speaking and writing (e.g. those whose jobs require them to deal with English speakers on the phone and write emails). For students, other skills might include note taking and problem-solving.

8.2.2 Designing new materials

In designing new materials or adapting existing ones, authentic texts should be used if possible. This means that for a reading lesson, the ideal texts for the materials designer to use are real examples of what the students will be expected to read. For a writing lesson, a real text should ideally be used as an example for the students. The materials designer should consider where the text comes from and who wrote it. Also important is the original communicative and sociocultural purpose of the text (Mishan, 2005 in Bocanegra-Valle, 2010). If you as a teacher want students to learn to write academic texts, using a news article for the materials will not be advisable, because the style and genre of the news article are very different from academic texts. In Chapter 7 we saw the experience described by Noguera-Díaz and Pérez-Paredes (2019) in relation to a course for seamen working in military submarines. They note that although it would have been preferable to use real military documents to build their corpus, this was not possible. Because of security concerns, they were not given access to these documents. As a result, they were forced to build their corpus using articles from military magazines. This created a limitation with their corpus and thus with any materials based on it.

However, if the proficiency level of the students is low, there may also be difficulties in using authentic texts. Although authentic texts are valuable in that they provide the learners with exposure to real language of the type that the learners will have to use, they are problematic in the sense that the language of the texts may be too difficult for the learners. Equally, simplified texts have advantages and disadvantages. Their benefit is that they focus on language features that the learners need to learn. However, they don't give the learners experience in coping with real texts of the type they need to cope with in their studies or job (Bocanegra-Valle, 2010). Another serious problem is that by simplifying the language, the materials designer can inadvertently distort both the meaning and the language features.

Another important consideration for teachers when they produce their own materials (Bocanegra-Valle, 2010) is that teachers need to ensure a good match between students' linguistic knowledge and that required by the oral or written discourse to be included in the materials. Equally, students should be able to cope with the content level of texts included in the materials, while teachers should also make sure their language learning goals match the students' discipline or workplace.

Task 8.1

> Think back to a time when you adapted materials from other
> sources. Which of the techniques mentioned above did you use?
> Give examples.

8.3 Evaluating materials

How can ESP teachers evaluate existing materials? Chan (2009) suggests that after reviewing relevant research about the genre, register, discipline or skills that are to be taught, the materials designer should use or make a checklist for evaluating self-designed materials or ready-made ones. Sometimes there are existing checklists for materials evaluation. However, Chan found that existing checklists can lack the detail that is needed to assess suitability and authenticity. Another shortcoming of some checklists is that they focus on practical concerns like cost and general pedagogical concerns like topic and what kind of learners, rather than on linguistic aspects of the materials.

Chan therefore designed more specific checklists for materials evaluation. Such checklists can be used to identify gaps in self-designed materials or ready-made ones. The materials designer can then address these gaps by supplementing the materials. As an example, below we consider Chan's checklist which she developed for evaluating materials to teach business meetings. In developing her checklist, Chan considered both pedagogical concerns and how well the materials handled the teaching of appropriate discourse. These are summarised in Table 8.2

Table 8.2 Checklist for evaluating materials to teach business meetings (based on Chan, 2009)

Checklist to evaluate pedagogical concerns	Checklist to evaluate how well the materials teach business meetings discourse
1. Needs analysis: Is the content relevant to business? Does it draw on the business experience of job-experienced learners?	1. Do the materials present both language for communicating business ideas and language to establish social relationships?
2. Learning objectives: Do the learning objectives relate to general or specialised language knowledge? Do they relate to general or professional communication skills?	2. Are the different roles of chairs and participants made clear?
3. Teaching approach: Do the exercises and activities help learners practise the language and strategies used in meetings? Do they mirror real-life business situations?	3. Do the materials provide practice in using different levels of formality?
	4. Is appropriate language to signal the opening and closing of different phases of meetings included?
4. The language models in the materials: Are authentic materials or samples of authentic spoken language used?	5. Is appropriate language for signalling topic opening and closing included?
	6. Do activities help learners practise skills necessary for cross-cultural meetings?

Task 8.2

Look at some materials that you recently used. These could be ones you designed yourself, or ones you adapted from elsewhere, or ones you used from a textbook. Design some questions you would use to evaluate the materials. Include at least one question relating to pedagogy and one question relating to the specific discourse (context in which the language will be used; genre and register) that the materials aim to teach.

8.4 Some examples of materials design

This chapter has noted the benefit of basing materials on learner needs and preferably on a needs analysis. It has also stressed the importance of relying on research to support the materials development. Also important is using authentic texts in developing materials. In this section we examine three studies describing materials design. These show varying degrees of use of needs analysis, use of research and use of authentic texts.

The first study, by Edwards (2000), describes materials developed under the difficulties of limited time and an inability to use authentic texts as part of the materials. The second study, by Candlin et al. (2002), describes materials drawing on a research project to improve Legal English education for second language speakers of English. Importantly, the authors draw on authentic texts as well as on research. The third study, by Malicka et al. (2019), describes materials design based on an in-depth needs analysis, including observation in the workplace and interviews with in-service professionals also in the workplace. It also includes authentic texts. By drawing on a needs analysis and authentic texts, it represents the ideal for ESP materials development.

Edwards (2000) describes how the author, an English language teacher in Germany, designed materials specific to the needs of officials at a German bank. The author had limited time for materials development, as teaching this course formed only a small part of his work. He therefore added and made alterations to ready-made materials. Edwards' course had several aims. The first aim of the materials was to improve the students' spoken English used in business meetings and negotiations. Secondly, the materials aimed to support the students in giving presentations using different kinds of graphs and charts. Thirdly, the materials also aimed to improve the German officials' skills of writing reports, reading short articles related to banking, as well as listening to language used by native speakers in meetings and 'small talk'. The author wanted to improve the speaking confidence of the students when they interacted with speakers of English as a first language.

To address these aims, Edwards designed information-gap and opinion-gap exercises where students had to pool information in order to complete financial statements and reports. The author also designed materials where the German officials needed to organise jumbled sentences to develop familiarity with the discourse patterns of business meetings, business negotiations and 'small talk'. He used cloze tests of articles of interest for students to develop vocabulary. He recorded class discussions and role plays simulating a meeting or negotiation. The students evaluated their own performance in these simulated meetings.

This reliance on simulated meetings reflects a limitation of Edwards' study in that because of confidentiality concerns, for the most part he was not able to draw on authentic documents or record real meetings. However, he was able to use authentic interview transcripts for role plays.

A second study by Candlin et al. (2002) describes how the authors evaluated existing Legal English textbooks. The authors describe how materials in these textbooks can be adapted, and how further new materials can be developed. The authors collected 56 textbooks on Legal English. Problematically they found that most of these had been written for students who spoke English as a first language. The books were either focused on legal content with little on legal language, or on general writing principles (i.e. not specific to law), or on stereotypical (non-research-based) ideas of what legal language is like. For law teaching to second language speakers of English, they suggest several ways these materials could be adapted. Firstly, they suggest customising the materials for second language students of English by using more effective rhetorical devices (e.g. authentic writing samples, examples, diagrams, figures etc.). They propose embracing a more language and discourse-based approach by grounding the materials in discourse analysis of authentic legal language (task-based exercises, questions for discussion and review, role-playing, simulations). Candlin et al. adopted a genre-based approach, and considered important genres that law students need to read or write, either as students or later in their professional lives (e.g. case brief, problem-solving essay, legal letter). Unlike some of the textbooks, they suggest a focus on discourses of the law (the norms and values of the legal community), not on legal content. Finally, instead of focusing either on language or on law, as some of the textbooks did, they recommend development of materials that integrate language and the law.

The third study by Malicka et al. (2019) examines real-life tasks that hotel receptionists carry out. An aim of the study was designing a pedagogic unit. Authentic data was used to gain insights, through needs analysis, into what tasks were often done by hotel receptionists, the language associated with these tasks, task difficulty and task sequencing. Qualitative data was collected, which included ten semi-structured interviews with five hotel receptionists and five tourism students in internships, together with three observations at three hotels in Barcelona. Seven categories were analysed in the interview data; these included the target tasks, task frequency, task difficulty and linguistic difficulty. Based on their findings, a needs analysis-based pedagogic unit was developed, which consisted of three oral tasks for different difficulty levels on the topic of 'Overbooking'. Overall, this study demonstrates how real-life tasks can be used to design pedagogic ones. Their study suggests that the target tasks and their frequency can be employed in curriculum design to select tasks and to decide the order in which they should be presented to the learners. In addition, the findings on task difficulty can also be applied to the pre- and post-task stages of a task, which translate to what vocabulary should be taught beforehand (pre-task) and how to apologise to a customer because of overbooking (post-task).

In summary, if possible, the materials designer should draw on research, on an analysis of students' needs and on authentic texts. However, as we can see in Edwards' (2000) study, for materials development teachers sometimes have very limited time, and may not have access to authentic texts.

8.5 Summary of the chapter

In summary, this chapter has shown how an ESP approach to materials development shares many principles with materials development for general English teaching. However, there are a number of differences. Firstly, ESP materials need to place greater emphasis on specificity, on learners' disciplinary and workplace speech events, genres and activities. They need to support learners in acquiring disciplinary or workplace values. Secondly, learners' specific needs should form the basis of materials in ESP. Materials should be based in the content of the discipline or workplace. Finally, features of disciplinary or workplace language (genre and register) should be given precedence.

The chapter has also considered the process of materials development. Ready-made materials need to be evaluated to assess their suitability for use. They can be adapted if necessary. Alternatively, new materials can be developed. Evaluation of materials should be based on existing research, as should adaptation of existing materials or development of new materials.

8.6 What should a teacher do after reading this chapter?

Consider the materials you are currently teaching as an ESP teacher. Evaluate the materials. Do they meet what you know about your students' needs? Do they use authentic texts? Do they integrate language teaching with the content of the students' discipline? Are there any studies that you can find on the language of the students' discipline? Are your materials genre-based? What changes could you implement to improve the materials?

Chapter 9

Assessment in ESP

┌─ **Pre-reading questions** ─────────────────┐

Before you start reading this chapter, think about the following:

1) Given what you know about the field of ESP, what key features do you expect will be associated with assessment in ESP?

2) If we want to measure the language proficiency of medical professionals or people working in business settings, is the use of generic language tests such as IELTS and TOEFL justified or not? What do you think?

└───┘

9.1 Introduction: why are specific purposes tests needed?

If we want to measure the language proficiency of medical professionals or people working in business settings, the use of generic language tests such as IELTS and TOEFL is not likely to be adequate. The reason for this is that these tests have been designed to test students who need English for academic purposes. They are not specific to any academic discipline. They are not designed to test English for any workplace.

To the first question above, regarding what key features you expect to be associated with assessment in ESP, from what you have learnt about ESP in this book, you might have answered that you expect the assessment to be specific to the learners' academic discipline or their workplace. In addition, as Douglas (2013, p.368) says, 'ESP programs require assessments that reflect the content and methodology of the ESP course, which are themselves based on an analysis of the target language use situation.' Thus, assessment in ESP, like assessment in any course, must test what the course has taught.

Think back to Chapter 2 where we discussed the necessity in ESP to be based on a careful analysis of students' needs. Once the teacher or researcher knows what the students' needs are for language in their discipline or workplace, this will tell them what the students need to be able to do at the end of the course. If we think back to the backwards design model of course design

(Wiggins & McTighe, 2005), which we considered in Chapter 4, we will remember that assessment, learning objectives, and teaching and learning activities must all be aligned. We can see that we should start with learners' needs and use them to work out what we want the learners to be able to do at the end of the course – the assessment tasks. This will tell us what our learning objectives should be, and what teaching and learning activities we should design to achieve these.

Figure 9.1 Alignment of student needs, assessment tasks, learning objectives, and teaching and learning activities

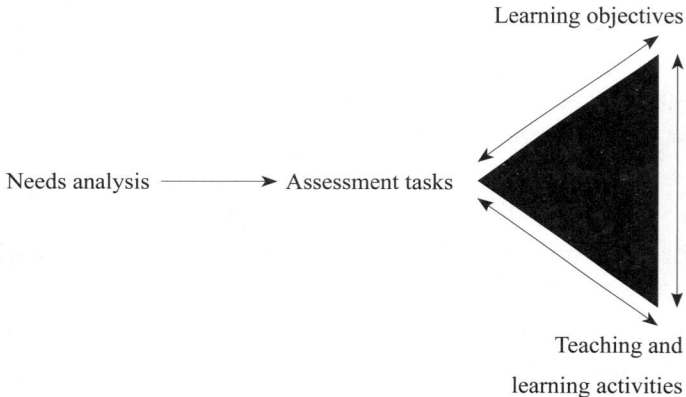

9.2 Authenticity of task

Douglas (2000, p.2) notes that an important aspect of ESP tests is authenticity of task. An authentic assessment task or test is one that can be expected in the target domain. That is to say, it is a task or test that learners need to do in their discipline or workplace. For example, students may be expected to write laboratory reports on their practical work if they are science students; they may be expected to write case studies if they are business students; they need to interact with patients if they are nurses; and they need to serve customers if they work in retail.

Task 9.1

Think of the ESP course you teach, or an ESP course you would like to teach. Think back to the learning objectives you set in Chapter 4. Write down your ideas for an assessment task that:

– is authentic to the discipline/profession

– aligns with one of the learning objectives you identified earlier

9.3 Specific purposes language and specific purposes background knowledge

We are all aware that language use varies with context. Just as the language we use in a job interview is different from the language we use when chatting to a friend, so the language of doctors talking to fellow medical professionals is more technical than the language that doctors use when talking to patients. In addition, the language of doctors is different from the language of air traffic controllers because different technical language is used, and it is based on a different body of content knowledge.

Specific purposes language is very precise. It uses technical lexis and specific patterns. There is also interaction between specific purposes language and specific purposes background knowledge. Users gradually come to learn the technical lexis and specific patterns of language while they are learning the background content knowledge (Douglas, 2013). Thus, their non-linguistic knowledge is linked with language knowledge. In addition to background knowledge, other non-linguistic factors such as body language, cues and symbols can have a big influence on the test takers' ability to do the test (O'Sullivan, 2012).

Because of this interaction between specific purposes language and specific purposes background knowledge, and because we adjust our language use depending on the context, assessment tasks should be embedded in disciplinary contexts. For example, Sabieh (2018) makes the point that testing nurses' vocabulary using a crossword puzzle would not test if they can use that vocabulary in a clinical context. Similarly, an assessment task to test if students can write emails, letters and memos will be more informative of learners' knowledge if it is embedded in real life scenarios related to a workplace context.

An example of the kind of knowledge that professionals need, and which may be neglected in assessment, is that medical professionals need to have pragmatic knowledge of the language to communicate effectively with patients. Studies such as Elder et al. (2012) and Staples (2015) have found that overseas-trained healthcare professionals may have cultural styles of communication that are different from those in the local context. This need for knowledge of interpersonal interaction is sometimes neglected in specific purposes tests. For example, the language criteria in a medical assessment (the Occupational English Test) neglected important features that are essential to communication for doctors (Jacoby & McNamara, 1999). Figure

9.2 shows the criteria used in the Occupational English Test.

Figure 9.2 Test criteria for Occupational English Test (OET) (Jacoby & McNamara, 1999)

Overall communicative effectiveness							
Near native flexibility and range	6	5	4	3	2	1	limited
Intelligible	6	5	4	3	2	1	Unintelligible
Even fluency	6	5	4	3	2	1	Uneven fluency
Complete comprehension	6	5	4	3	2	1	Incomplete comprehension
Appropriate language	6	5	4	3	2	1	Inappropriate language
Rich flexible grammar and expression	6	5	4	3	2	1	Limited grammar and expression

Task 9.2

Jacoby and McNamara (1999) found that doctors supervising migrant physicians complained about poor language proficiency despite their supervisees having passed the Occupational English Test. However, when they tested the migrant physicians using the Occupational English Test assessment, the doctors and Applied Linguist OET testers agreed in their assessments of the physicians' proficiency.

What does this suggest to you about the Occupational English

Test criteria? Are these criteria important to language specialists or to health professionals? What changes would you suggest?

Task 9.2 shows a gap between linguistic and professional assessment criteria. A number of studies (e.g. Elder et al., 2012) have suggested that the answer to this problem is that the criteria that are of significance to the discipline or profession and more importantly, the judgements of professionals, must be taken into account. To do this, criteria that disciplinary or professional communities use for judging communicative competence need to be identified. In ESP, these criteria are said to be 'indigenous' to the disciplinary or professional communities. Just as we regard people as indigenous to the country they come from, so the criteria recognized and used by experts in a discipline or professionals in a workplace can be seen as indigenous to that discipline or workplace.

A study by Elder et al. (2012) investigated what criteria clinical educators use to assess the spoken clinical communication of health professionals. They investigated this by asking 33 clinical educators from the professions of medicine, nursing or physiotherapy to assess a video of students or trainees from their profession interacting with a patient. The criteria that the clinical educators used are shown in Figure 9.3. If we compare this to current Occupational English Test criteria (Figure 9.2), we can see that criteria such as fluency and flexibility were not mentioned by clinical educators.

Figure 9.3 Indigenous criteria that clinical educators use to assess the communication of health professionals (Elder et al., 2012)

1	Affect	affective state; general emotion, mood
2	World view	personal beliefs based on culture etc.
3	Approach	attitude/sensitivity to patient's needs etc.
4	Manner	behaviour towards patient
5	Communication skills	eye contact & engaging with patient
6	Content	coverage of issues, clinical knowledge
7	Organisation	structure/sequence of tasks; process
8	Techniques	interactional tools/resources
9	Terminology	medical language, technical/lay terms
10	Nonverbal communication	e.g. eye contact, posture
11	Language	e.g. intelligibility, grammatical accuracy

Another study that identified indigenous criteria by asking professionals to judge the communicative competence of other professionals is one by Knoch (2014). This study sought to investigate the assessment criteria that pilots use when assessing the language ability of other pilots. Knoch wanted to validate the International Civil Aviation Organization rating scale which is used to assess pilots' and air traffic controllers' aviation English proficiency. To do this, 10 pilots listened to and rated testees taking aviation tests. The pilots also mentioned non-linguistic categories (such as technical knowledge) in addition to the linguistic ones (such as pronunciation and comprehension) which are part of the existing test.

Yet another study (Jacoby & McNamara, 1999) investigated the assessment criteria used by physics researchers practising their presentations to prepare for a conference. Figure 9.4 shows the qualities that were prized by the physics researchers. Which of these criteria would you use in assessing your students' abilities with oral presentations?

Figure 9.4 Assessment criteria used by physics researchers for oral presentations (Jacoby & McNamara, 1999)

1. Overall quality of the performance
2. Keeping to the time limit
3. Articulating the significance of the topic to the profession
4. Designing visuals to accompany the talk which are coherent and legible
5. Stating arguments and labelling visuals clearly
6. Stating information, arguments and rhetorical steps explicitly and completely
7. Avoiding verbosity
8. Making effective, convincing arguments
9. Maintaining accuracy of content
10. Avoiding linguistic errors
11. Delivering a technically polished performance (in terms of volume, rate, body positioning, management of the visuals)

9.4 Writing assessment tasks

What should we consider when we write ESP assessment

tasks? How do we go about writing them? Two elements of any assessment task are the **rubric** and the **prompt**. The rubric refers to information about how the assignment or test should be done and the prompt refers to the input to be processed to complete the task.

The rubric may include the objective of the assessment: describing what the task or each part of the task will assess, e.g. 'This is a test of your ability to identify the main points in a short lecture.' It may also describe the procedures for responding, e.g. 'Answer all the questions in complete sentences', 'Complete the table using information from the graph.' Finally, it can specify the task format, including the importance of each sub-task and distinctions between them, e.g. 'The questions relate to the case study materials provided', 'The writing task is based on your understanding of the text and so you should attempt section one first' (Douglas, 2000).

The prompt is a stimulus to the response to the task. This can be stated directly, e.g. 'Write an essay discussing the advantages and disadvantages of studying online during the pandemic.' A situation can also be presented as a prompt for the task, e.g. 'You have been asked by your school principal to investigate students' experience of using online teaching during the pandemic. Design a questionnaire and use it to survey the student body. Based on the results of your survey, write a report for your school, analysing the advantages and disadvantages and making recommendations for future use of online teaching methods.' Figure 9.5 provides an example of a prompt and rubric for a case study assignment for engineering students.

| Figure 9.5 | Example prompt and rubric for engineering case study |

Cyclones can have destructive and disruptive effects. One example was the damage and destruction in Tonga caused by Cyclone Gita in 2018. Another was Hurricane Dorian that struck the Bahamas in 2019. Cyclones can cause disruption to power systems, leading to effects like disruption of medical services and communications.	Prompt
Write a case study, choosing one such recent event for your case study. Analyse what made the pre-existing power system infrastructure vulnerable. Make recommendations for how it could be made more robust. You should ensure that your recommendations address the provision of emergency power immediately after a severe weather event.	Rubric

Good work will have:

- Clear and concise description of the case.
- Discussion and analysis of relevant issues or problems.
- Recommendations concerning improvements or avoidance of possible threats/problems.
- Use and critical evaluation of multiple sources.
- Referencing sources to support any statements made.

9.5 Summary of the chapter

This chapter has discussed the importance of assessment tasks being aligned with the analysis of student needs on the one hand, and with the learning objectives, and teaching and learning activities on the other. Secondly, the chapter has focused on the importance of ESP assessment tasks being authentic to the disciplinary/workplace context. ESP assessment needs to take account of criteria that are important to the discipline/profession. It also needs to take account of both specific purposes language and specific purposes content knowledge. Finally, this chapter has considered how language for specific purposes assessment should be framed.

9.6 What should a teacher do after reading this chapter?

Evaluate the assessments and tests that you use in your ESP course. Are they authentic to your students' discipline or workplace? Do they test the skills, genres or language that your ESP course teaches? Do you view them as related to your students' needs in their discipline or workplace?

Chapter 10

Conclusion

┌─ **Pre-reading questions** ─────────────────────┐

Before you start reading this chapter:

1) Make a list of what you feel are the most important
   features of English for Specific Purposes teaching.

2) Write down your thoughts on what aspects of English
   for Specific Purposes teaching make it most different
   from general language teaching.

└──┘

Key principles of English for Specific Purposes that have been discussed in this book

English for Specific Purposes teaching is different from general English language teaching, in the sense that it focuses on the language needs that students have in a particular domain such as their studies or work. This distinguishes them from students who have more general needs, which might include studying a language in order to go and live or travel in another country, or become better integrated with the speakers of the language. This book has considered a number of important principles of English for Specific Purposes.

Firstly, as Chapter 1 discussed, language teaching should be as specific as possible to the target discipline or workplace. This is because their studies or work is the reason learners are learning the language. So how the language is used in this specific context is the main interest they have in learning it. Learners often have limited time for language learning, so ESP tries to make the best use of this limited time.

Secondly and related to the first principle, Chapter 1 also notes that language teaching materials should be based in the content of the discipline or workplace. As stressed throughout this book, language use differs from context to context depending on the purpose of its use, on the audience and on how well the writer or speaker knows the reader or listener. So, use of disciplinary or workplace content aims to maximise the chances that the language taught is relevant to the discipline or workplace. However, although content material is used in ESP, it is important that teachers focus on teaching the language of the discipline or workplace, not the content material of the discipline or workplace.

Thirdly, central to ESP is a focus on learner needs, which was discussed in Chapter 2. Unlike in general English language teaching, learners' needs may be specific to groups and differ very widely between learners in different disciplines or workplaces, so finding out what learners' needs are enables learners to function in the target language in the target discipline/workplace.

Fourthly, because ESP teachers are not disciplinary or workplace experts, they need ways to find out what their learners' needs are. Chapter 3 discussed qualitative ways. The methods involve interviewing experts, observation in the target context and textual analysis of relevant texts. By these methods ESP teachers can also come to understand disciplinary or workplace values, and they and then learners can acquire these values.

Fifthly, the teaching context and the learners' needs should guide curriculum development in ESP. Teachers' needs for professional development should also be considered. These issues were discussed in Chapter 4.

A sixth important aspect of ESP is that, as discussed in Chapter 5, the approach selected to curriculum design should be one that is compatible with integrating the learning and teaching of content and language. For example, a grammar-based approach, where the curriculum is designed according to the grammatical structures being learnt, will not be appropriate. This is because although grammar is relevant to ESP students, this grammar must be learnt in the context of the disciplinary or workplace language.

A seventh principle of ESP, also addressed in Chapter 5, is that the focus of teaching should be on disciplinary or workplace speech events, disciplinary or workplace texts and disciplinary or workplace activities. The needs analysis will guide the teacher in this. For example, as discussed in this book, health professionals engage in spoken interaction with their patients, so this is a speech event that ESP teachers of trainee nurses or doctors can focus on. The discourse in these contexts is complex, so as much as possible teachers should draw on needs analysis and studies of language use in the context done by prior researchers.

As was discussed in Chapter 6, ESP teachers should identify and teach disciplinary and workplace genres. Teaching should give attention to organisation of disciplinary or workplace texts (move analysis) and also the values, purposes and audiences of such texts. Once again, prior studies can be very useful for ESP teachers, who are often very busy and unable to undertake this analysis.

Chapter 7 discussed the use of corpora to identify the register features of disciplinary or workplace language. Attention should be given not only to the language features, but also to how they achieve the values and purposes of the discipline or workplace.

A further principle (discussed in Chapter 8) is that teaching materials should integrate the language and the content of the learners' discipline. ESP materials need to emphasise specificity, learners' disciplinary or workplace speech events, and key genres and activities. They also need to support learners in acquiring disciplinary or workplace values.

A final principle of ESP (discussed in Chapter 9) is that ESP testing and assessment should ensure that assessment tasks align with students' needs, with the learning objectives, and with the teaching and learning activities. Significantly, testing and assessment should focus on specific purposes language and specific purposes content knowledge, and draw on criteria that are important to disciplinary experts and those in the workplace.

Glossary

Academic skills Reading, writing, speaking, note taking etc.

Authentic assessment A task or test that can be expected in the target domain, i.e. the learners' discipline or workplace.

Authenticity Real texts or contexts that are found in a discipline or workplace.

Collaboration with discipline specialists Disciplinary teacher and language teacher work together outside of the classroom for language classes that prepare students to learn the disciplinary subject in English.

'Common core' approach The idea that there are skills and forms of language that are generic across disciplines, professions and purposes.

Contextual factors Circumstances of a particular context; aspects that are unique to a group, a community, a society or an individual.

Corpus A collection of texts. This can either be a general corpus, which tries to include representative texts from a wide range of genres and contexts. Or it can be a specialised corpus, which includes texts of a particular type (e.g. student assignments) or genre (e.g. student essays).

Curriculum The instruction that learners get during their education.

Disciplinary culture The beliefs, attitudes and norms of the discipline. These are reflected in the use of language in the discipline.

Genre Written texts or speech events that are related to particular purposes and audiences. Examples of written genres are essays, reports, emails etc. and examples of spoken genres are lectures, conversation, nurse–patient interaction etc.

Genre awareness The insight that a writer or speaker has about how to use the genre flexibly in response to their own purposes, and their awareness that genres are not unchanging.

Genre stages A similar concept to moves, stages indicate the organisation of a text.

Indigenous assessment criteria Assessment criteria that are recognised and used by experts in a discipline or professionals in a workplace can be seen as indigenous to that discipline or workplace.

Lacks What the learner still needs to learn about the specific purposes language, in order for them to become successful in their discipline or workplace.

Language logs A diary of learners' language-related activities.

Learning goals A teacher's long-term intentions of teaching.

Learning objectives Specific language that the learners will know or specific language-related abilities that the learners will achieve by the end of the course. These are observable, measurable actions or capabilities.

Move analysis An analysis of the meanings expressed in a particular genre.

Moves pieces of a text that perform a particular purpose or express a particular meaning. Together the moves in a text fulfil the overall purpose of the text.

Necessities The knowledge and use of language that are necessary for the learners to succeed in their discipline or workplace.

Needs analysis An analysis of what learners need the language for: What writing or speaking do they need to do in the language? What purposes do they use the language for?

Notional-functional curriculum A curriculum based on a consideration of what learners need to communicate in the language (e.g. greeting, introducing, making requests, apologising etc.)

Observer paradox To what extent do observing and studying the event change the participants' behaviour.

Pedagogical genres Short texts such as recounts, discussions and procedures, which are common in primary school classrooms.

Prompt A stimulus to the response to an assessment task. For example, it can describe a situation or problem and ask the test taker to respond to the situation or problem.

Qualitative methods Data obtained by observation rather than measurement or counting. Typical qualitative methods are interviews, observation, documents, narratives, and student or teacher journals.

Register The linguistic features (vocabulary and grammar) of the language used by a particular group of people or for different purposes (e.g. academic writing compared with fiction, or lectures compared with casual conversation).

Rubric Information about how an assignment or a test should be done.

Sociocultural context The way that language use is linked to the society, the culture, and the event or purpose for which the language is being used.

Specificity Related to a particular discipline, workplace, subject or context.

Specific purposes The limited field in which learners will use the language, usually their academic discipline or workplace. Examples are Business English, Medical English and Engineering English.

Speech functions The functions the speaker is attempting to fulfil such as questioning, apologising, refusing, inviting, making small talk etc.

Team-teaching Disciplinary teacher and language teacher prepare classes and teach the class together.

Theme-based curriculum A curriculum in which language activities are embedded in a theme drawn from the learners' discipline. An example is a theme on magnetism to learn the language of physics.

Transcription An interview or other spoken event that has been written down.

Triangulation The use of multiple methods or sources of information to investigate a context or phenomenon. This increases reliability if the different methods support each other.

Wants Learners' perceptions of the language and other factors they need for success in their discipline or workplace.

References

Auerbach, E. (1995). The politics of the ESL classroom: Issues of power in pedagogical choices. In J. W. Tollefson (Ed.), *Power and Inequality in Language Education* (pp.9-33). Cambridge: Cambridge University Press.

Bacha, N. N., & Bahous, R. (2008). Contrasting views of business students' writing needs in an EFL environment. *English for Specific Purposes*, *27*(1), 74-93.

Bancroft-Billings, S. (2020). Identifying spoken technical legal vocabulary in a law school classroom. *English for Specific Purposes*, *60*, 9-25.

Basturkmen, H. (2010). *Developing Courses in English for Specific Purposes*. Basingstoke: Palgrave Macmillan.

Basturkmen, H. (2014). LSP teacher education: Review of literature and suggestions for the research agenda. *Ibérica*, *28*, 17-34.

Basturkmen, H., & Bocanegra-Valle, A. (2018). Materials design processes, beliefs and practices of experienced ESP teachers in university settings in Spain. In Y. Kırkgöz & K. Dikilitaş (Eds.), *Key Issues in English for Specific Purposes in Higher Education* (pp.13-27). Cham, Switzerland: Springer.

Basturkmen, H., & Shackleford, N. (2015). How content lecturers help students with language: An observational study of language-related episodes in interaction in first year accounting classrooms. *English for Specific Purposes*, *37*, 87-97.

Benesch, S. (1999). Rights analysis: Studying power relations in an academic setting. *English for Specific Purposes*, *18*(4), 313-327.

Benesch, S. (2001). *Critical English for Academic Purposes: Theory, Politics, and Practice*. London: Routledge.

Berkenkotter, C., & Huckin, T. N. (1993). Rethinking genre from a sociocognitive perspective. *Written Communication, 10*(4), 475-509.

Bhatia, V. K. (2004). *Worlds of Written Discourse: A Genre-Based View.* Shanghai: A&C Black.

Biber, D., Connor, U., & Upton, T. A. (2007). *Discourse on the Move: Using Corpus Analysis to Describe Discourse Structure.* Amsterdam: John Benjamins Publishing.

Biber, D., Johansson, S., Leech, G., Conrad, S., & Finegan, E. (1999). *Longman Grammar of Spoken and Written English.* London: Longman.

Bloom, B. S. (Ed.) (1956). *Taxonomy of Educational Objectives: The Classification of Educational Goals – Handbook I: Cognitive Domain.* London: Longmans, Green and Co.

Bocanegra-Valle, A. (2010). Evaluating and designing materials for the ESP classroom. In M. F. Ruiz-Garrido, J. C. Palmer-Silveira & I. Fortanet-Gómez (Eds.), *English for Professional and Academic Purposes* (pp.141-167). Amsterdam: Rodopi.

Bocanegra-Valle, A., & Basturkmen, H. (2019). Investigating the teacher education needs of experienced ESP teachers in Spanish universities. *Ibérica, 38*, 127-150.

Bosher, S., & Stocker, J. (2015). Nurses' narratives on workplace English in Taiwan: Improving patient care and enhancing professionalism. *English for Specific Purposes, 38*, 109-120.

Cameron, R. (1998). A language-focused needs analysis for ESL-speaking nursing students in class and clinic. *Foreign Language Annals, 31*(2), 203-218.

Candlin, C. N., Bhatia, V. K., & Jensen, C. H. (2002). Developing legal writing materials for English second language learners: Problems and perspectives. *English for Specific Purposes, 21*(4), 299-320.

Chan, C. S. C. (2009). Forging a link between research and pedagogy: A holistic framework for evaluating Business English materials. *English for Specific Purposes, 28*(2), 125-136.

Chan, C. S. C. (2021). Helping university students discover their workplace communication needs: An eclectic and interdisciplinary approach to facilitating on-the-job learning of workplace communication. *English for Specific Purposes, 64*, 55-71.

Chan, M. (2014). Communicative needs in the workplace and curriculum development of Business English courses in Hong Kong. *Business and Professional Communication Quarterly, 77*(4), 376-408.

Charles, M. (2014). Getting the corpus habit: EAP students' long-term use of personal corpora. *English for Specific Purposes, 35*, 30-40.

Cheng, A. (2006). Understanding learners and learning in ESP genre-based writing instruction. *English for Specific Purposes, 25*(1), 76-89.

Cheng, A. (2007). Transferring generic features and recontextualizing genre awareness: Understanding writing performance in the ESP genre-based literacy framework. *English for Specific Purposes, 26*(3), 287-307.

Cheng, W., Lam, P. W. Y., & Kong, K. C. C. (2019). Learning English through workplace communication: Linguistic devices for interpersonal meaning in textbooks in Hong Kong. *English for Specific Purposes, 55*, 28-39.

Christison, M., & Murray, D. E. (2021). *What English Language Teachers Need to Know, Volume III: Designing Curriculum* (2nd ed.). London: Routledge.

Coxhead, A., & Demecheleer, M. (2018). Investigating the technical vocabulary of plumbing. *English for Specific Purposes, 51*, 84-97.

Cowling, J. D. (2007). Needs analysis: Planning a syllabus for a series of intensive workplace courses at a leading Japanese company. *English for Specific Purposes, 26*(4), 426-442.

Cutting, J. (2012). English for airport ground staff. *English for Specific Purposes*, *31*(1), 3-13.

Dong, J., & Lu, X. (2020). Promoting discipline-specific genre competence with corpus-based genre analysis activities. *English for Specific Purposes*, *58*, 138-154.

Douglas, D. (2000). *Assessing Languages for Specific Purposes*. Cambridge: Cambridge University Press.

Douglas, D. (2013). ESP and assessment. In B. Paltridge & S. Starfield (Eds.), *The Handbook of English for Specific Purposes* (pp.367-383). Chichester, West Sussex: Wiley-Blackwell.

Dudley-Evans, T., & St John, M. J. (1998). *Developments in English for Specific Purposes: A Multi-Disciplinary Approach*. Cambridge: Cambridge University Press.

Edwards, N. (2000). Language for business: Effective needs assessment, syllabus design and materials preparation in a practical ESP case study. *English for Specific Purposes*, *19*(3), 291-296.

Edwards, T. (2019). English for cleaners: Developing and trialling an ESP lesson for learners with low-level English proficiency. *TESOLANZ Journal*, *27*, 44-56.

Elder, C., Pill, J., Woodward-Kron, R., McNamara, T., Manias, E., Webb, G., & McColl, G. (2012). Health professionals' views of communication: Implications for assessing performance on a health-specific English language test. *TESOL Quarterly*, *46*(2), 409-419.

Evans, S. (2012). Designing email tasks for the Business English classroom: Implications from a study of Hong Kong's key industries. *English for Specific Purposes*, *31*(3), 202-212.

Ferguson, G. (2001). If you pop over there: A corpus-based study of conditionals in medical discourse. *English for Specific Purposes*, *20*(1), 61-82.

Flowerdew, J., & Wan, A. (2010). The linguistic and the contextual in applied genre analysis: The case of the company audit report. *English for Specific Purposes*, *29*(2), 78-93.

Gibbons, P. (2015). *Scaffolding Language, Scaffolding Learning* (2nd ed.). Portsmouth, NH: Heinemann.

Grosse, C. U. (2004). English business communication needs of Mexican executives in a distance-learning class. *Business and Professional Communication Quarterly*, *67*(1), 7-23.

Harwood, N. (2005). 'We do not seem to have a theory … The theory I present here attempts to fill this gap': Inclusive and exclusive pronouns in academic writing. *Applied linguistics*, *26*(3), 343-375.

Henry, A. (2007). Evaluating language learners' response to web-based, data-driven, genre teaching materials. *English for Specific Purposes*, *26*(4), 462-484.

Henry, A., & Roseberry, R. L. (2001). A narrow-angled corpus analysis of moves and strategies of the genre: 'Letter of Application'. *English for Specific Purposes*, *20*(2), 153-167.

Huhta, M., Vogt, K., Johnson, E., & Tulkki, H. (2013). *Needs Analysis for Language Course Design: A Holistic Approach to ESP*. Cambridge: Cambridge University Press.

Hutchinson, T., & Waters, A. (1987). *English for Specific Purposes: A Learning-Centred Approach*. Cambridge: Cambridge University Press.

Hyland, K. (2002a). Authority and invisibility: Authorial identity in academic writing. *Journal of Pragmatics*, *34*(8), 1091-1112.

Hyland, K. (2002b). Specificity revisited: How far should we go now? *English for Specific Purposes*, *21*(4), 385-395.

Jackson, J. (2005). An inter-university, cross-disciplinary analysis of business education: Perceptions of business faculty in Hong Kong. *English for Specific Purposes*, *24*(3), 293-306.

Jacoby, S., & McNamara, T. (1999). Locating competence. *English for Specific Purposes, 18*(3), 213-241.

Jasso-Aguilar, R. (1999). Sources, methods and triangulation in needs analysis: A critical perspective in a case study of Waikiki hotel maids. *English for Specific Purposes, 18*(1), 27-46.

Johns, A. M. (1997). *Text, Role, and Context: Developing Academic Literacies.* Cambridge: Cambridge University Press.

Johns, A. M. (2011). The future of genre in L2 writing: Fundamental, but contested, instructional decisions. *Journal of Second Language Writing, 20*(1), 56-68.

Jordan, R. R. (1997). *English for Academic Purposes: A Guide and Resource Book for Teachers.* Cambridge: Cambridge University Press.

Knoch, U. (2014). Using subject specialists to validate an ESP rating scale: The case of the International Civil Aviation Organization (ICAO) rating scale. *English for Specific Purposes, 33,* 77-86.

Koester, A. (2010). *Workplace Discourse.* London: A&C Black.

Lam, P. W. Y., Cheng, W., & Kong, K. C. C. (2014). Learning English through workplace communication: An evaluation of existing resources in Hong Kong. *English for Specific Purposes, 34,* 68-78.

Long, M. H. (2005). *Second Language Needs Analysis.* Cambridge: Cambridge University Press.

Lu, Y.-L. (2018). What do nurses say about their English language needs for patient care and their ESP coursework: The case of Taiwanese nurses. *English for Specific Purposes, 50,* 116-129.

Malicka, A., Guerrero, R. G., & Norris, J. M. (2019). From needs analysis to task design: Insights from an English for specific purposes context. *Language Teaching Research, 23*(1), 78-106.

Martin, J. R. (1984). Language, register and genre. *Children Writing: Reader, 1,* 21-30.

Martin, J. R. (1985). Process and text: Two aspects of human semiosis. In J. D. Benson & W. S. Greaves (Eds.), *Systemic Perspectives on Discourse, Vol 1: Selected Theoretical Papers from the 9th International Systemic Workshop* (pp.248-274). Norwood, NJ: Ablex.

McLaughlin, E., & Parkinson, J. (2018). 'We learn as we go': How acquisition of a technical vocabulary is supported during vocational training. *English for Specific Purposes*, *50*, 14-27.

Michaels, S. (1981). 'Sharing time': Children's narrative styles and differential access to literacy. *Language in Society*, *10*(3), 423-442.

Michigan Corpus of Upper-Level Student Papers. (2009). Ann Arbor, MI: The Regents of the University of Michigan. Accessible at http://micusp.elicorpora.info/.

Mishan, F. (2005). *Designing Authenticity into Language Learning Materials*. Bristol: Intellect.

Nesi, H. (2012). Writing in the disciplines. In L. Clughen & C. Hardy (Eds.), *Writing in the Disciplines: Building Supportive Cultures for Student Writing in UK Higher Education* (pp.55-73). Bingley: Emerald Group Publishing.

Nesi, H., Gardner, S., Thompson, P., & Wickens, P. (2008). *British Academic Written English Corpus*, Oxford Text Archive, http://hdl.handle.net/20.500.12024/2539.

Noguera-Díaz, Y., & Pérez-Paredes, P. (2019). Register analysis and ESP pedagogy: Noun-phrase modification in a corpus of English for military Navy submariners. *English for Specific Purposes*, *53*, 118-130.

Northcott, J. (2001). Towards an ethnography of the MBA classroom: A consideration of the role of interactive lecturing styles within the context of one MBA programme. *English for Specific Purposes*, *20*(1), 15-37.

O'Sullivan, B. (2012). Assessment issues in languages for specific purposes. *The Modern Language Journal*, *96*(Focus Issue), 71-88.

Park, S., Jeon, J., & Shim, E. (2021). Exploring request emails in English for business purposes: A move analysis. *English for Specific Purposes*, *63*, 137-150.

Parkinson, J. (2000). Acquiring scientific literacy through content and genre: A theme-based language course for science students. *English for Specific Purposes*, *19*(4), 369-387.

Parkinson, J. (2017a). The student laboratory report genre: A genre analysis. *English for Specific Purposes*, *45*, 1-13.

Parkinson, J. (2017b). Teaching writing for science and technology. In J. Flowerdew & T. Costley (Eds.), *Discipline-Specific Writing: Theory into Practice* (pp.95-113). London: Routledge.

Parkinson, J. (2020). Use of personal pronouns in science laboratory reports. In D. R. Gruber & L. C. Olman (Eds.), *The Routledge Handbook of Language and Science* (pp.150-163). London: Routledge.

Peacock, M. (2002). Communicative moves in the discussion section of research articles. *System*, *30*(4), 479-497.

Perry, B., & Stewart, T. (2005). Insights into effective partnership in interdisciplinary team teaching. *System*, *33*(4), 563-573.

Sabieh, C. (2018). English for specific purposes (ESP) testing. In J. I. Liontas (Ed.), *The TESOL Encyclopedia of English Language Teaching, Volume VIII*. Hoboken, NJ: Wiley-Blackwell.

Schleppegrell, M., & Achugar, M. (2003). Learning language and learning history: A functional linguistics approach. *TESOL Journal*, *12*(2), 21-27.

Sinclair, J. M. (Ed.) (2004). *How to Use Corpora in Language Teaching*. Amsterdam: John Benjamins Publishing.

Spack, R. (1988). Initiating ESL students into the academic discourse community: How far should we go? *TESOL Quarterly*, *22*(1), 29-51.

Spence, P., & Liu, G.-Z. (2013). Engineering English and the high-tech industry: A case study of an English needs analysis of process integration engineers at a semiconductor manufacturing company in Taiwan. *English for Specific Purposes*, *32*(2), 97-109.

Staples, S. (2015). Examining the linguistic needs of internationally educated nurses: A corpus-based study of lexico-grammatical features in nurse–patient interactions. *English for Specific Purposes*, *37*, 122-136.

Staples, S. (2019). Using corpus-based discourse analysis for curriculum development: Creating and evaluating a pronunciation course for internationally educated nurses. *English for Specific Purposes*, *53*, 13-29.

Swales, J. M. (2004). *Research Genres: Exploration and Applications*. New York: Cambridge University Press.

Tardy, C. M. (2011). Genre analysis. In K. Hyland & B. Paltridge (Eds.), *The Bloomsbury Companion to Discourse Analysis* (pp.54-68). London: Bloomsbury.

Tomlinson, B. (2010). Principles of effective materials development. In N. Harwood (Ed.), *English Language Teaching Materials: Theory and Practice* (pp.81-108). New York: Cambridge University Press.

Warren, M. (2013). "*Just spoke to …*": The types and directionality of intertextuality in professional discourse. *English for Specific Purposes*, *32*(1), 12-24.

Wiggins, G., and McTighe, J. (2005). *Understanding by Design* (2nd ed.). Alexandria, VA: Association for Supervision & Curriculum Development.

Wollman-Bonilla, J. E. (2000). Teaching science writing to first graders: "Genre learning and recontextualization". *Research in the Teaching of English*, *35*(1), 35-65.